To all who continue to learn and who give
that opportunity to others

Publisher's acknowledgements

The publisher gratefully acknowledges the help of all the organisations and companies who kindly gave approval to show screen shots of their products or web sites.

Contents

Supporting
on-line learning

John Hurley

 Learning Partners

Published by Learning Partners
Suite 4 Marquis House
2 North Street
Winchcombe
Gloucestershire GL54 5LH

Telephone/Fax 01242 604060
email *lp.books@argonet.co.uk*
www.lpbooks.co.uk

© Learning Partners 2001
ISBN 1 899692 07 X

Printed by Biddles
Unit 24 Rollesby Road
Hardwick Industrial Estate
Kings Lynn
Norfolk PE30 4LS

Introduction

This book is about both precept and practice in on-line learning. It argues for intelligent management of the process of on-line learning, so that the opportunities are not used to dilute the quality of the educational experience for either students or staff. It provides an understanding of the educational context for guidance and support and for on-line learning and shows how the two can be integrated to develop good practice for teaching and tutoring on-line.

Like it or not, we are at the beginning of the much heralded revolution in computer-based learning. Of course there have been many false dawns for this over-hyped concept, but it is at last happening. The reasons are simple: the advances in network technology in the 1990s give us a suitable infrastructure. The rethinking of the role of computers in education, combined with a move from teacher-led to student-managed learning in post-16 education has provided a framework for educational practice.

We now contemplate a wide range of on-line educational opportunities. On-line materials can provide additional resources for conventional, institutionally based learning and for distributed and distance learning. It can also provide new ways of delivering these provisions. The discussion contained in this book is therefore relevant for all post-16 education whether in schools, colleges, universities or in the community.

The argument of this book is that the new age will provide huge educational resources, held electronically, which will be available to both institutionally based programmes and through a proliferating number of on-line educational providers. In either case the central educational process will be the learning activities carried out by the student. These will be formally structured by teaching – or on-line teaching materials – but the key role will be the support and development of learning through tutoring.

Tutoring in these contexts will contain elements of what is normally considered teaching (running discussions and group activities) and various forms of guidance and support activities. The book argues that there is an appropriate paradigm of tutoring for learner development, which defines a variety of tutoring arrangements to meet the needs of students within new and old forms of course delivery.

It is essential that guidance and support are integrated into the design and delivery of learning programmes, rather than being simply a bolt-on extra. The aim should be to create an integrated learning environment, even where parts or all of that environment are on-line.

For institutionally based provision this principle reflects the shift from teaching to tutoring, which is a consequence of the development of learner-focused programmes. In many institutions there are established frameworks for guidance and support. Institutionally-based learning programmes can draw upon these existing resources, but as we move away from institutions towards virtual campuses, community provision and lifelong learning through on-line provision, we see that there is a need to develop on-line, workplace or community equivalents for these guidance and support structures.

There are no particular solutions that are universally applicable. What is appropriate to distance-learning provision is not necessarily the best way to support institution-based students. Some distance-learning provisions have established extensive face-to-face guidance and support networks which students value. Students themselves have very different learning needs and learning styles which must be taken into account. There are, however, distinct guidance stages and support requirements that any effective system must acknowledge. It is the recognition of the underlying principles and requirements which, in combination with particular delivery strategies, produce the specific solutions which are most effective. This book addresses these issues.

Hennessy, Flude and Tait (1999)

BTEC (1993)

Summary   The book divides into three themes. The first is developed in Chapters 1 and 2, which give an overview of the development of on-line learning and the guidance and support process, showing the desirability of an integrated approach.

The second theme is developed in Chapters 3 and 4, which consider the development of guidance and support in relation to on-line learning. Chapter 3 concentrates on developments in educational institutions and Chapter 4 on developments in distance and distributed learning using a case study approach. This chapter also considers the benefits and risks of the globalization of education which is occurring as a result of the on-line revolution.

The final theme concerns the implementation of the guidance and support process. Chapter 5 considers the crucial (and often overlooked) requirements of initial guidance for on-line learning. Chapter 6 looks at tutoring and the provision of academic guidance. Chapter 7 considers the organization of support and some of the personal skills required of tutors.

Chapter 8 provides a brief afterword that summarises the key conclusions of the book, through a programme for implementation.

The development of on-line learning

The use of computers in education has been growing since the early 1980s but has not, until recently, made any fundamental impact. Recent advances in network technology have created new possibilities for the use of information and communications systems as learning resources and as learning environments. The success of on-line learning depends on the integration of technology into a coherent learning programme.

A revolution in learning

The phrase 'on-line learning' encompasses a very broad vision of educational provision. It subsumes within it a wide variety of approaches and situations, from a college student using instructional software on a classroom-based computer, to a home-based learner, engaged in analytical discussion in the virtual coffee bar of a trans-national, internet-based learning environment.

It is not a particularly new vision. In the late 1980s, experiments were taking place in sixth form, further and higher education to exploit the emergent computer-based technology. In East Anglia, Clifford Dixon, a college principal, was converting classrooms to resource centres and attempting to educate students around clusters of computers. Government-funded projects aimed to develop teaching packages for classrooms, or for distance learning. In the early 1990s the Higher Education Funding Council for England (HEFCE) introduced funding for its Teaching and Learning Technology Programme.

HEFCE (1995/6)

None of these early developments made much impact. They were limited by what computers could achieve, and how information could be shared, by a restricted understanding of how information technology could be used and, as a consequence of these, by software which generally aimed at instruction rather than supporting the learning process. Most early developments were irrelevant to the central process of education, as it was then seen, and remained at best marginal to mainstream practice.

If this is true, why do we now stand on the threshold of a revolution in education? The answer is twofold.

Over the period of experimentation with on-line learning the latent power of linking computers in networks has been realised, and with the development of the Internet a vast, global educational resource has been created. As access to this resource has become easier, it has expanded exponentially. Over this same period of time there has been change in the dominant conception of the education process, from emphasis on instruction and inputs to greater weight being placed on learning and outcomes. A spin-off has been the development of software which seeks to stimulate the educational process, rather than just provide subject-specific instruction and testing.

At the leading edge of these developments are the virtual learning environments which utilise the power of information networks to simulate the functions and activities of an educational institution, with little regard for geographical distance, time barriers or national frontiers. The result, very shortly, will be permanently accessible global institutions of education. This may be seen as a potentially liberating development, or as potentially Orwellian, according to view. A short discussion of the benefits and dangers is included later in this book. What is certain is that it will happen and that the revolution is upon us.

www.learn2.com

Figure 1 Learn2.com – globally available education

The developing concept of a learning programme

It is not so long ago that the understanding of the educational process was largely that teachers taught a syllabus which was examined. This model of education emphasises teaching input, the acquisition of subject knowledge and the testing of that knowledge. It persists as an influential model of education, not least in the minds of some journalists and politicians, but it has lost ground to another view. Over the last two decades there has been a significant shift of educational focus from one that was based upon what was taught, described in the syllabus, to one that is based upon what is learned, described in a learning programme.

The alternative view places learning at the centre. Around this are assembled the teaching and learning experiences that develop knowledge and understanding, subject-related skills, learning skills and higher intellectual abilities (like critical reasoning). These are reinforced through assessment systems that measure the range of learning outcomes. In this model the learner is not seen as a passive recipient of knowledge through teaching, but as an active agent in the learning process, in partnership with the teacher.

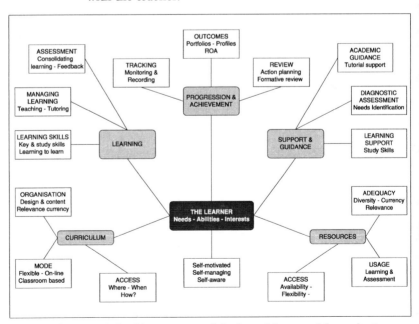

Figure 2 A model of learner-centric teaching and learning

In order to be active participants, learners must be helped to be able to manage their contribution to their education independently of the teacher. The motivation for learners is the greater control they enjoy in relation to how and when they learn, and their enhanced ability to achieve their learning goals. This model represents a change in emphasis from teaching to learning, and also lays greater stress on outcomes – the achievements resulting from learning.

The differences between the models are to some extent ones of degree. Good teaching has always involved large elements of student participation and active student learning. In emphasising achievement through student learning, good quality inputs of teaching or instruction remain vital. Where the learner-centric view differs from the syllabus and examination model is in laying greater emphasis on the range of activities which make up teaching, learning and assessment. It develops the role of teacher simply from instructor to that of provider of guidance and student support. The greater variety of experience in teaching, learning and assessment which this view promotes is unified by the notion of the learning programme.

Elements of a learning programme   A modern unified learning programme can be seen to have six elements.

Teaching and teaching materials include those elements of instruction which address the knowledge base, assist understanding or demonstrate skills. In addition to lecturing or related teaching activities, teaching can be conducted through textbooks, instructional materials in open and distance learning or computer-based instructional materials.

Learning and learning resources include all of those activities which allow the acquisition and development of knowledge, understanding and skills. Learning can occur individually or in groups, but the essential characteristic is that the learner, not the teacher, is the active agent. Learning materials are, therefore, those that do not seek to instruct, but allow the practice of intellectual, learning and practical skills. These range from primary book resources or CD-ROMs, to resource materials held on computer networks (intranets or the

Internet) to materials that allow skills to be practised in workshop or laboratory situations.

It is immediately apparent that this last aspect of learning is not always easily simulated on-line (although in some cases it can be) and that on-line learning may need to be situated within a broader educational context as part of the learning programme.

www. polemicpublishing. co.uk

Figure 3 The title page of an information resource on CD-ROM

Assessment Effectively designed assessment should work at three levels.

Diagnostic assessment should establish learners' starting points by identifying suitable programmes and learning needs that may require support. For example, does a student have sufficient mathematical ability for the calculations required in an engineering module? Is support required through a maths workshop or a problems class? Diagnostic assessment can also be used to check or self check the development of learning and identify areas where knowledge or understanding is insufficiently developed. It lends itself readily to simple on-line testing, although attempts at more comprehensive assessments of learning styles, maturation or capability have been less successful.

Formative assessment is concerned with tasks which monitor the development of knowledge, understanding and/or skills and feeds that information back to the student to enable them to improve their performance. Formative assessment is vital to a learner-centric model of education and is an essential basis for student guidance and support.

Summative assessment measures the learning outcomes, in terms of knowledge, understanding and skills. It may be conducted in a number of ways, not just through examinations, but the purpose is to identify and record the achievement of learning outcomes.

Whilst this is familiar to most teachers, it is far from clear that all the problems in running effective assessment regimes are resolved. In higher education review reports, for example, a lack of rigour, consistency or clear purpose in assessment which fails to measure achievement of intended outcomes is often reported. *QAA (1999)* However education is delivered, the design and process of assessment is vital to the success of the learning programme.

The familiar tripartite structure of teaching, learning and assessment does not encompass all the elements of the learning programme. Three further elements are equally vital to its success.

Academic guidance encompasses a wide range of activities, from providing students with the information to make informed choices on their programme to feeding back through written comment on assessment or by recorded discussion information that will help a student to learn more effectively. Guidance is also concerned with helping students understand the learning programme and developing the range of learning and intellectual skills required.

Learner management is closely related both to academic guidance and to teaching. It involves the structuring of learning for individual students, monitoring and tracking their progress and identifying problems and difficulties. Central processes may include periodic review (leading to academic guidance) and action planning where students can identify goals for their learning and assessment.

Student support entails meeting the needs of students identified through diagnostic assessment or through learner management. It may involve help integrated into the learning programme, specific additional help (for example, with the necessary maths for a programme) or supplementary help (such as a separate learning skills package).

These six elements of the learning programme can be organised into two clusters, as shown in the table below.

The teaching/learning cluster	The guidance/support cluster
Teaching – providing instruction and direction in learning	Academic guidance – helping students to develop their learning by the provision of information and feedback
Learning – the acquisition of knowledge and skills, undertaking independent student-managed study	Learner management – reviewing progress and planning learning
Assessment – measuring the achievement of learning outcomes	Student support – structured skills support for student achievement

Table 1 Elements of a learning programme

Within contemporary learning programmes there is a further emphasis shift from input to outcome and from teaching to learning which has already been noted. This is the greater emphasis placed on academic staff in their guidance and support roles or as managers of learning. *Saunders (2000)* As Saunders says in his companion book, it is a shift from '*the sage on the stage, to the guide on the side*'. In more prosaic language it represents a shift from those activities normally associated with teaching towards those normally associated with tutoring. The term 'tutoring' is used here to subsume academic guidance, learner management and support, rather than any particular tutoring system. Tutoring then becomes a framework through which teaching can be conducted.

The changing context of post-16 education Alongside the technological revolution and the shifting understanding of the educational process, there have been significant political and social changes in our requirements for the post-16 education system. The most evident of these has been the aspirations of all recent governments to significantly broaden access to further, higher and continuing education. Total participation in post-16 education has increased substantially. At the same time, there has been a greater concern with efficiency in the education system, thus ensuring that students are retained for the duration of a programme (or are enabled to transfer to an alternative and more suitable one) and successfully attain their final qualification. Finally, recent governments have reduced the resources they are prepared to devote to continuing education by cutting financial support to students and reducing the unit of resource.

The educational policies intersect in an interesting way with the shifts in our view of the educational process. The requirements for efficiency link closely to the stress on outcomes and guidance and support strategies. The squeeze on funding has posed problems for educational managers, however, which they have attempted to resolve by increasing the size of teaching groups or increasing staff teaching hours. This ultimately works against the ability to deliver the additional elements of the teaching programme, and has led in further education to poor morale, overwork and burnout amongst staff.

One reason why education managers look at on-line learning with some interest is that it appears to offer them some possibilities for delivering mass further and higher education, with their restricted resources. *Saunders (2000)* Saunders draws attention to the limitations of this view, but in colleges and universities more use can certainly be made of on-line strategies in providing information to free up the resources to deliver better guidance and support. In turn, learner-centric approaches to education provide a framework within which on-line learning can be made successful.

Developing on-line learning programmes The development of learner-centric programmes provides an ideal context for the development of on-line learning within institutions. However, the impact of on-line learning is likely to be even more dramatic upon distance learning systems. This recognises that information technology can be integrated with learning programmes at several different levels. The National Council for Educational Technology (NCET) has *NCET (1988)* suggested a three-fold classification of levels:
- *Centre-based provision* takes place within an established educational institution. The development

of on-line materials is seen as part of a strategy of resource-based learning or supported self-study, for full- and part-time students. Typically this has led to the development of learning resource centres or computer-based learning workshops. These are characterised as resource-based learning and computer-assisted learning.

- *Local provision* is made available by a provider within a local area, typically through drop-in learning centres, community-based learning centres, workplace learning centres or at home. There are many variants of these patterns which may be characterised as distributed learning.
- *Distance learning* is organised by national providers who offer individual study opportunities, generally at home or in the workplace.

At each level we are part way through an evolution from paper-based resources to electronic resources, to networked information and communications technology becoming the dominant form in which learning materials are made available. On-line provision can be seen, at each level, as:

- *An addition to existing provision.* In many cases on-line provision is organised to augment and expand a programme that continues to be taught through lecture, seminar and workshop or laboratory activities.
- *An integrated part of a diverse provision that offers a range of learning experiences.* This goes one stage further, providing more opportunities for learning from the on-line materials and more opportunity for tutoring in the taught programme.
- *A mode of delivery.* We have reached a point where whole programmes can be offered on-line using a range of communications technologies. This is particularly useful for distance or community-based provision.

Technological and educational developments taken together have increased the real educational possibilities of information technology. Most importantly they have allowed information and computer technology to become more than a bolt-on to the learning process (or a poor substitute for it) and to become an integrated part of a learning programme. How well the technology is integrated depends on how well the programme is designed and the relevance of what is provided on-line.

At its simplest, a network may bring together programme information, teaching materials, learning resources and perhaps support materials. These are frequently organised as web pages on an intranet, although there are many other ways course – or programme – specific materials can be organised. Most course teams start with those materials to which students refer frequently – handbook information, learning outcomes, assessment tasks, assessment and marking criteria. Beyond the basic information, essential or scarce learning materials might be made available. Some thought needs to be given to what the students need to know or practise. Materials that relate to common areas of difficulty or enable students to work through particular problems are very useful.

On-line material may provide some degree of inter-activity to create a 'learning environment' related to the programme. This may be given by teaching software, self assessment tests, or examination revision programs. It might be provided by a prescribed research task using resources provided on-line or on a CD-ROM.

Some interactive support might be provided by e-mail links to tutors, and students can possibly claim and evidence key skills or subject skills on-line. It is essential that the resource and learning materials are planned to contribute meaningfully to the programme. For instance, students might be directed towards handouts relating to a topic which is being dealt with in lectures and seminars, and these may be accompanied by further resources – reading material from the web, a teaching programme or a self test programme.

Integrated learning environments become essential if on-line learning becomes the chosen means of delivery for distance learning. This integration will, at the minimum, encompass programme information, teaching and assessment materials, learning resource materials and some on-line help and guidance. It may also extend to the use of on-line video resources, interactive demonstrations, or conferencing activities.

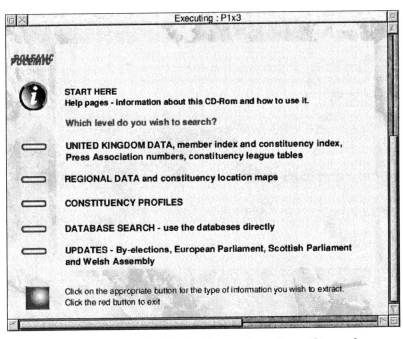

Figure 4 Page from British Parliamentary Constituencies showing the information available for research.

Software such as Top Class or Symposium is used for this purpose. First Class is used by the Open University and a number of further education colleges for distance and community provision.

Learning environments can be further developed through the creation of virtual campuses *(see Figure 5 overleaf)*. These use software which, as well as providing access to information, teaching materials and resources, also provides interactive areas for on-line guidance and support, group working and student or staff discussion. Whilst a virtual learning environment can exist as a community within an orthodox educational setting, they have a particular relevance for the delivery of distance learning programmes.

The advantage of such systems for distance learning is that they introduce opportunities for formal support structures to be integrated into the on-line teaching programme and for informal peer contact to occur in chat rooms or working groups.

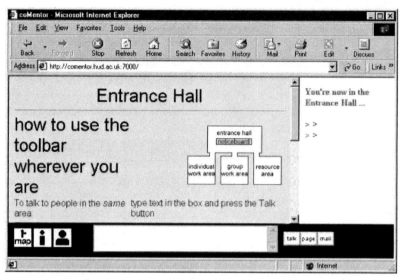

Figure 5 CoMentor homepage – a simple virtual campus

http:// comentor.hud.ac.uk/ Whether we are looking at on-line provision in conjunction with an established institution-based programme or the provision of a learning programme wholly on-line, good provision has some similar characteristics. Successful provision:

- *is based on users' real needs* – wordprocessing allowed students to present their work more effectively and simply, e-mail allowed them to contact their friends, the web allows them to access information. Good on-line educational provision should make learning more straightforward.

- *engages students with the process of learning* by providing appropriate tools, skills and information to support student directed activity. Good on-line provision puts the student at the centre and allows them to undertake those activities which help them manage their own learning. This might be to research new information, to try to understand an area they find difficult or to check their knowledge, understanding or skills acquisition.

- *offers a coherent and integrated learning environment* and a good student experience, irrespective of how much of the study programme is provided on-line.

The costs of on-line learning lie principally in the development, authoring and presentation of materials and their subsequent maintenance and updating. The potential savings are in the delivery of the resources. In the present climate of cost savings, the temptation may be to develop, or buy 'off-the-peg', learning programmes which address the teaching–learning–assessment cluster without adequately dealing with the guidance–management–support aspects. This would reverse the good practice in contemporary learning programmes of making teaching and tutoring equal partners in developing learning. Certainly within educational institutions, as on-line learning becomes more widely used, the provision of guidance and support becomes more central to the learning process. As learning is distributed through networks, the challenge will be to ensure that all elements of contemporary learning programmes are developed.

Integrating guidance and support into on-line learning programmes

This chapter has suggested that modern teaching approaches increasingly use guidance to help self-directing learners to learn effectively. This reflects a shift of emphasis from teaching to tutoring in the provision of learning programmes. Teaching tends to be directive, helping students to acquire new information and skills. Tutoring tends to be more reflective, encouraging the review, management and consolidation of learning.

The technology that is developing for on-line learning facilitates the creation of integrated learning environments, whether wholly on-line or integrating on-line elements with face-to-face delivery. If on-line learning is to be part of an integrated learning programme, academic guidance and support must be addressed. Since guidance and support are key elements of contemporary learning programmes, it is essential that they are integrated into on-line provision from the outset, not bolted on afterwards. To the list of criteria for successful on-line learning provision it is necessary to add a further requirement which will guide future development. Successful provision:
- *recognises that there should be an adequate and integral framework of guidance and support.*

Summary

- On-line learning is revolutionizing the provision of education.
- Good on-line provision complements the developing emphasis on learning as the centre of the educational process.
- Successful learning programmes are concerned not only with teaching, learning and assessment, but also with academic guidance, learner management and student support.
- The focus on learning necessarily integrates guidance, support and learner management, through tutoring.
- Tutoring includes teaching and guidance and support functions.
- On-line learning can be developed either within traditional institutions or for new patterns of distributed and distance learning.
- Learning environment software can allow the development of virtual campuses on-line.

The next chapter examines the meaning of guidance and support in relation to learning programmes and identifies activities and approaches which are applicable to on-line learning.

The guidance and support process

Guidance and support can be readily integrated into learning environments. It is important, however, that the forms of guidance and support which are integrated are based upon an up-to-date model of the guidance process. This chapter provides a discussion of the essential aspects of guidance and support in relation to on-line learning and enables those providing on-line opportunities for their students to make informed decisions on strategies for integrating support.

Helping students to succeed

The development of on-line educational provision will contribute to the extension of educational opportunity. The emphasis on lifelong learning entails a substantial widening of access to further and higher education, particularly in respect of the age of students and the variety of ways in which they will be studying. It is not enough, however, to 'throw open the portals' of education. What is offered as an open door can, all too easily, become a revolving one as students drop out from or fail their course. This is undesirable at every level – in the use of resources and for the experience of students and staff. The expectation should be that once admitted students will successfully complete their studies.

HESA (1999)

A recent study shows that around 80% of students on taught higher education courses will successfully complete their studies, with the majority of students who do not complete leaving during the first year of their programme. Retention in further education and for distance learning is generally lower than retention in higher education.

In higher education there is a substantial variation between types of institution and individual institutions within each type in their ability to retain students. *'The wide variation between institutions with a similar intake causes some overall concern. The reports suggest that institutions with the capacity to monitor student attendance and academic performance, and who identify and give academic guidance to students in potential difficulty, were*

QAA/HEFCE (1998)

more able to retain students irrespective of their intake.'

Not all student populations have the same characteristics and the needs of students may vary considerably. Education providers may also offer very different levels of support. Best practice suggests that guidance and support should be matched to the needs of the student population and be sufficient for that population. This applies particularly to on-line and distance learning. In order to deliver an effective support strategy for on-line learning it is necessary to consider first the requirements of the student population. If these needs are to be met, then we must understand the various elements that make up guidance and support, and how they contribute to the organisation of the whole learning programme.

Models of the guidance and support process

Hurley, Smith and Hurley (1995)

There is a well established model of guidance through education, which is organised around three phases of students' experience – prior to entry, on programme and on exit. Originally proposed by the FEFC, Learning Partners has developed a modified version of this model which clarifies the guidance and support roles at each stage (Table 2).

Pre-entry/at entry	On programme	For completion
Initial guidance for the educational programme	Planning the learning programme	Progression guidance
Assessment of learning skills/ prior learning	Assessing, recording and feeding back achievement	Summative assessment and recording achievement
Assessment of learning and support needs	Formative review	
	Monitoring and tracking progression	
	Providing learning skills and key skills support	
	Setting expectations and managing learning	

Table 2   The stages and activities of guidance and support

There is much confusion about the nature of guidance in education and at least four different guidance processes are involved in this model.

Educational guidance is involved at the pre-entry and entry stage, and again before completion with guidance on educational or vocational progression. Educational guidance is concerned with the choices students make about their area, mode and level of study and their intended career progression. It can help students to identify which programme and which provider most closely meets their needs.

Educational and careers guidance should:
- inform intending learners of all available opportunities
- base its information on the objectives, capabilities and needs of the client
- offer impartial advice.

Employment Department (1991)

In 1986 the Unit for the Development of Adult Continuing Education (UDACE) published *The Challenge of Change* which defined seven core activities for educational guidance:
- informing
- advising
- counselling
- assessing
- enabling
- advocating
- feeding back.

UDACE (1986)

Quite clearly, although such a programme may be impartial, it is not professionally detached from the client. It has a positive orientation to student access and success. In practice, the goal of impartiality is hard to achieve. Education providers may offer guidance which is compromised by the desire to recruit; independent careers and education guidance providers may be compromised by the need to fill targets set by their sponsors and government.

Academic guidance is the principle form of provision whilst a learner is on-programme. Academic guidance is committed to enabling students to achieve their objectives. It is neither impartial nor detached.

Academic guidance should be:
- based on the client's objectives, capabilities and needs
- committed to the achievement of the agreed learning goals

- supportive of the development of the student's abilities and learning skills.

Within the framework of specified learning outcomes the core activity of academic guidance is to help the student manage their learning by:
- planning their approach to learning and assessment tasks
- monitoring student activity and progress
- tracking student achievement
- providing feedback on student performance, for example, through formative feedback on completed assessment tasks
- helping the student to review their progress towards the agreed and planned goals
- enabling students to improve their achievement.

Academic guidance may be used to maintain or raise the level of students' ambitions, ensuring that they undertake appropriately challenging tasks. Academic guidance is also closely related to learner support and may take on a number of student support roles by:
- helping students through any difficulties they encounter during their course
- identifying areas of learning difficulty for which support can be provided
- encouraging students to remain 'on course' to achieve the learning contract

Hurley, Smith and Hurley (1995)
- providing teaching in learning or key skills.

There are a number of competing paradigms of academic guidance, widely used in education, which are explored later in this chapter. Some of these concepts seem to be particularly appropriate to on-line learning.

Personal guidance and counselling is the third dimension of guidance used in the guidance model. It is more difficult to characterise personal guidance because a residential college will necessarily be more involved in personal guidance than a distance learning organisation. There is also a long amateur tradition in personal guidance which is at odds with more recent professionalization (for example, of counselling) or statutory regulation of financial advice.

Broadly, personal guidance:
- is based upon the interests of the learner

- deals with issues which are not directly academic
- is impartial and detached within a professional advisory or counselling framework.

Personal guidance and counselling covers a wide range of supplementary advisory and support services which can deal with student problems, the most common of which are:
- financial
- legal
- personal and relationship.

Where support for housing, financial, legal, relationship and childcare difficulties is provided, these can do much to support and enable students to remain on programme. By their nature, such services may rely on personal contact (to meet regulatory body or professional standards). Personal guidance and support is not typically offered by distance learning providers. Although there are expert systems for some areas of personal support, the preference for personal contact means that these guidance services are unlikely to be provided on-line, at least by education providers.

Learner and study support is the last dimension of the guidance and support model. Learner support provides practical help to enable students to succeed. It is concerned with the development of those skills which learners need to succeed at any level of learning, from basic communication skills to advanced research skills. As such, it may be involved at any stage of the guidance process, although it is a particularly strong partner for

Hurley (1994)   academic guidance. Learner support is:
- based upon the needs of the learner
- committed to successful outcomes.

Learner support will generally offer a range of services but will most often be involved:
- at entry stage in the diagnosis of learning support needs
- in the provision of support for basic skills and higher level learning skills
- in some systems, the development of key skills
- in developing inclusive learning strategies and support for people with disabilities or learning difficulties.

Learner support is heavily interventionist in attempting to develop skills to facilitate student achievement. It contains explicit teaching functions, though it does not necessarily have to be delivered through formal teaching or a tutorial or workshop. For example, it is seen by many academic tutors as a supplementary function to academic guidance, and much academic guidance may be involved in helping students to develop study/learning skills.

The inclusive learning functions may extend to ensuring that students with disabilities get the aids they need for using information technology. Whilst all of these functions are equally essential to on-line learning, it is not possible to deliver all of them on-line. The assessment of needs may often require personal contact, and the provision of support may need designated helpers in the workplace or the community.

On-line learning may require some integrated learning support to help students develop the IT skills they need to benefit from the programme. This may include initial tutorial materials for the equipment and software and subsequent technical and academic support on-line.

Paradigms of academic guidance and support

Hurley, Smith and Hurley (1995)

There are a number of paradigms of academic guidance. An explanation of these helps to highlight those which may be translated to on-line usage and illustrate the strengths and limitations of each. It should be remembered that what has been called the tutoring role is not identical to a tutorial system, which is only one way in which academic guidance can be delivered.

The personal tutorial paradigm remains the most common conception of guidance and support in post-16 and higher education. It is a somewhat amorphous model, mixing elements of educational guidance (for progression), academic guidance and personal guidance. The origins of the personal tutor lie with institutional responsibilities to be *in loco parentis,* and it is essentially based on personal knowledge and contact. This tends to promote a great deal of variability and becomes an essentially adult–child relationship which is not really suitable for adult students. It is not, therefore, a suitable model for on-line learning.

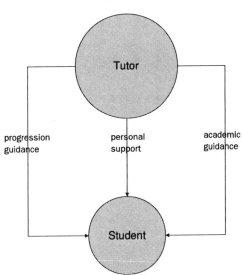

Figure 6 The tutor–student relationship in personal tutoring

The action planning paradigm is limited to academic guidance and centres on the management of student learning, concentrating on setting and reviewing goals, tracking and monitoring student progress and recording achievement. The approach is a highly focused one and can be delivered equally through personal contact or on-line. As a very process-orientated model, it lends itself to translation to on-line tutoring. As an essentially manager-managed relationship, however, it does not promote student autonomy very strongly. It is less proactive than other models because it does not make student support an integral aspect of the guidance process.

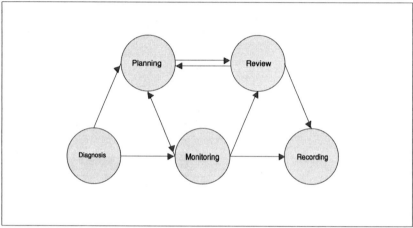

Figure 7 The action planning model of academic guidance

The learning development paradigm encompasses both academic guidance and learning support. This model stresses a more proactive form of academic guidance than the action planning approach, with greater emphasis on improving student skills and developing learning. As part of that development the model includes a greater encouragement to self-management by the learner. The process of review and action planning is less an end than a means to an end of learner development. The process-based elements of this model lend themselves readily to on-line adaptation and the effective integration of teaching and tutoring also lends itself to on-line adaptation. The more developmental

Asynchronous communication such as e-mail allows a discussion to take place over time. aspects may require some degree of personal contact by an academic guide, a tutor or perhaps a trained workplace mentor. Personal academic tutoring can take place on-line using asynchronous communication, or in realtime perhaps using live video-links. Although the integration of support elements means that this model is not the most easily translated to on-line usage, it is the most student focussed and comprehensive.

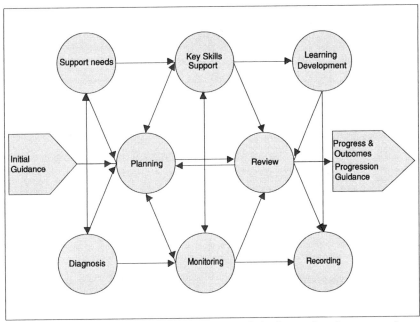

Figure 8 The learner development model of academic support and guidance

Guidance and support roles There are a number of roles that may be required on- or off-line which are concerned with ensuring that students can tackle the learning programme successfully. These are the essential activities of tutoring which include:
- directing and managing learning
- providing academic guidance and learning skills development
- providing basic and study skills support, dealing with learning difficulties and needs.

According to how the learning programme is organised, these roles can be fulfilled in a number of different ways. Where on-line learning is part of an established institution-based provision, existing structures might be adapted to meet students' needs. A greater use of on-line facilities might be sought, however, to increase the accessibility and consistency of tutoring and support. In other situations, particularly where there is a wide range of individual learners in a variety of remote situations, it may be necessary to deliver guidance and support wholly on-line.

In other situations it may be possible to deliver guidance through designated centres. In community settings learning centres may be established as a focus for guidance and support, or support might be organised in workplaces where programmes are vocationally relevant. This may give rise to new support roles, particularly those of the workplace mentor.

Finally, the technology of virtual campuses facilitates the development of peer support in a rather more formal sense than in face-to-face learning. The virtual coffee bar may be a far more serious and learning-orientated place than its real equivalent in colleges and universities.

These roles and their development will be discussed in later chapters.

Some issues of good practice in guidance and support

However support is organised, it must still deliver the essential principles of effective guidance and support to ensure learning outcomes. There must be a recognition of good practice in the conduct of guidance and support. Some of these principles of practice will be applicable to all on-line provision, some may arise only for longer qualification courses.

The first issue is one of confidentiality. If students are tracked and monitored, and they disclose information about themselves, this is confidential. Confidential information should be covered by an on-line privacy policy, which ensures that information is not passed on or used for other purposes and that it is secure.

Policies on when and how to refer need to be established. If a student is seen to be having problems with work or diagnostic assessment of a need is made, then it may be desirable to refer to more specialist help.

Such a referral should always be made with a student's permission and through clear procedures. Tutors should be able to handle most front-line problems, but also know when referral is appropriate.

Tutoring should ensure equity and access. This may mean that tutoring resources are not a simple per capita provision. A system which provides two hours of tutorial review per student as a working entitlement may need to have the capacity to spend further time with selected students when necessary to ensure that they are enabled to achieve satisfactory outcomes.

As was noted earlier in this chapter, academic guidance is a commitment to helping students achieve success. There are occasions when a tutor will be an advocate for a student (because they know that illness or personal circumstances have created difficulties for the learner) or may help self-advocacy by the learner (for example, by informing the student of how best to conduct an appeal). Such activities are a necessary part of a learner-centred approach, but do not necessarily fit easily into a highly systems-driven approach to education, or into those where there is no face-to-face contact. Advocacy and effective self-advocacy may be central to the needs of students with disability or disadvantage, thereby ensuring equity and accessibility.

Summary

- Appropriate guidance and support provision helps retention and enables student success.
- The guidance process from initial contact to exit involves different levels and types of guidance and support.
- Educational guidance, academic guidance, personal guidance and study support all contribute to success at relevant stages.
- Of the three paradigms of academic guidance and support, two are best suited to on-line learning.
- The action planning paradigm facilitates on-line tracking of student progress and learner management.
- The learner development paradigm facilitates the linking of teaching and guidance roles.
- These models can be delivered through a variety of on- or off-line patterns of tutoring.
- However guidance is delivered, it should recognise best practice in respect of confidentiality, referral and equal opportunity.

The next two chapters examine some strategies for delivering guidance and support on-line both in institutions and through distance learning.

Three

Guidance and support strategies for on-line learning in educational institutions

The development of on-line learning environments as a part of mainstream education is opening new and richer possibilities for self-managed learning. Institutions will initially be able to build on their existing guidance and support strategies and the new technologies will offer some further delivery options. In the medium-term new strategies will be required. Many students, however, will find that more traditional patterns of delivery and support meet their needs best.

The poverty of computer-based teaching

Adapt (1999)

A survey carried out in the autumn of 1999 showed that the majority of programmes delivered wholly on-line in further education were related to information technology. These programmes tend to be simply developments of the highly structured instruction-based approaches that characterise computer training. A high proportion of these courses were short and offered little more than basic technical support.

Anyone who has comparative experience of observing teaching in post-16 education will know that the teaching of IT results often in dull, student passive sessions, working from whole group instruction or a programmed tutorial. The problem stems fundamentally from the design of the operating systems and software that are most widely used, which do not lend themselves to acquisition of operating rules as in a language. As a result it is difficult to operate a consistent syntax to develop and extend powers of communication. The lack of consistency and the stress on features hidden in a complexity of options and preferences work against transparency and promote a 'learn each programme separately' approach.

There are operating systems which are easier to use and which have a stronger consistency in the interface allowing quicker facility with new packages. These have, however, fallen back in educational use against the onslaught of cheap 'industry standard' solutions. Whilst this does promote a standard for educational computing, it is not a wholly adequate standard and large numbers of people of all ages continue to find computer use frustrating.

Davies (2000)

The mechanical approach to computer learning does perhaps account for the relatively low educational worth of much of the inherited software which seeks to give instruction. There are some highly innovative programmes, particularly in technical areas, which work through interaction and experiment, but much instructional software is as dull as the average 'learn wordprocessing' teaching session. American studies of computer-based learning have suggested that children develop fewer skills using learning technology than through other teaching. Over the last decade the principle positive development in educational software has been to create more open-ended programs which slot into existing teaching areas. These are much more educationally relevant but need to be highly supported by teachers if they are to be effective.

On-line developments in education

A most important recent development has been the introduction of intranets within educational settings which create their own environment (often using a programming language called HTML – the language of the Internet). These can, in principle, run on any operating system, if it has the appropriate web browser software, and if well executed offer a simple and consistently easy to use interface. Intranets are very well adapted to the storage and retrieval of information, but if you want to run programs which manipulate this information, like databases, spreadsheets and wordprocessors, you are reliant on software packages running on the operating system.

Intranets have made a big impact, not to deliver whole learning programmes on-line, but as a tool for enriching existing provision. Since their strength is the retrieval and presentation of information, they are well suited to the independent learning of material that might otherwise be given through instruction. They also usually provide a gateway to the much larger range of resources found on the Internet. This approach dovetails neatly with the contemporary development of learning programmes. It potentially allows a reduction in time spent conveying information and more time to be spent on interpretation and developing learning and intellectual skills.

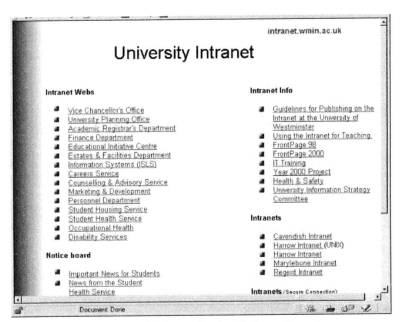

intranet.wmin.ac.uk

University Intranet

Intranet Webs

- Vice Chancellor's Office
- University Planning Office
- Academic Registrar's Department
- Finance Department
- Educational Initiative Centre
- Estates & Facilities Department
- Information Systems (ISLS)
- Careers Service
- Counselling & Advisory Service
- Marketing & Development
- Personnel Department
- Student Housing Service
- Student Health Service
- Occupational Health
- Disability Services

Notice board

- Important News for Students
- News from the Student Health Service

Intranet Info

- Guidelines for Publishing on the Intranet at the University of Westminster
- Using the Intranet for Teaching
- FrontPage 98
- FrontPage 2000
- IT Training
- Year 2000 Project
- Health & Safety
- University Information Strategy Committee

Intranets

- Cavendish Intranet
- Harrow Intranet (UNIX)
- Harrow Intranet
- Marylebone Intranet
- Regent Intranet

Intranets (Secure Connection)

Document Done

Figure 9 University of Westminster intranet page

Another factor is that if we enrich the learning programme and reduce fixed lecturing time in favour of more time devoted to supervised and supported independent learning, then it is possible to introduce much more flexibility in the times at which education is delivered. This may not yet mean much at school level, but in further and higher education it would allow more flexibility to meet student needs and use resources more efficiently.

Developing strategies for support and guidance

If current developments in on-line learning within institutions are essentially enriching more traditional learning programmes, then it may seem that, in principle, existing guidance and support structures, if they are adequate, will provide an appropriate framework. Indeed, as students spend more time obtaining information from computer databases, teachers should have more time to devote to tutorial functions – academic guidance, learner management and support.

One difficulty is that resource pressures on managers may tempt them to 'claw back' time saved from teaching functions, without recognising the need for adequate learning management if students are to learn independently – particularly at sub-degree level.

The resources vs. quality debate

Many education managers have supported the contemporary notion of a learning programme, not because it is educationally superior, but because it is more effective at retaining students and helping them complete their course. At the forefront of their concerns are efficiencies and savings in teaching costs which have led to higher workloads for teachers. It is likely that the development of on-line learning will be seen as a way of further reducing teacher contact and therefore teacher costs.

The counter argument is that education has to be not only efficient but effective, and that effectiveness can be measured not only in retention and completion but also in the quality of outcomes and student experience. This means that we need to use teaching resources where they make most impact – not in giving information, but in helping students to use and analyse the information and acquire the higher levels of understanding. This will be achieved not by using on-line learning to make savings on teacher costs, but by using the time saved to change teachers' role towards learning management.

Greater flexibility, however, will inevitably strain any guidance and support structure. For example, if a member of academic staff makes themselves available for an hour, after they have delivered a weekly lecture which all students attend, in which they provide guidance and support, then what happens if the content is placed on the intranet and students access this in the evenings or remotely? Inevitably existing frameworks will need to evolve to accommodate the greater flexibility that is possible.

As teaching becomes more plural and less structured, the provision of academic guidance and support will need to become more structured. Monitoring student learning and intervening to help make that learning effective is essential to student-driven systems. Fortunately, the new technologies do not just raise problems, they offer lines of solution. There are effective analogues in the new virtual worlds of education to many elements of traditional support structures. A common front-line guidance provision in universities is the allocation of time by academic staff when they offer 'open door' guidance and advice. Whilst this is not a very efficient way of providing structured tutorial support, it is effective at dealing with minor problems and queries and proffering quick guidance and advice. But it does require tutors and students to be in the same location at the same time – a requirement that may lead to frustration on both sides. It is not surprising that the open door is increasingly being supplemented or replaced by e-mail tutoring. Broadband communications will increasingly allow virtual face-to-face contact using electronic cameras irrespective of location.

Broadband communications allow very high rates of data transmission.

So effective short-term strategies will build upon established guidance and support frameworks. These will need to be adapted to meet the new demands, but should benefit from greater investment of time. There is a need to make them more structured and more proactive, which will ensure that they benefit from the new opportunities available from the technology. Some suggestions of how these developments might work are given in the next section. The FERL web site provides an excellent resource base for current practice.

www.ferl.co.uk

Figure 10 Homepage from the FERL web site

Short-term strategies for support and guidance The most effective response to the development of on-line learning within conventional learning programmes is to augment current frameworks with some of the provisions required to meet the demands of greater flexibility and to exploit some of the new opportunities given by the available technologies. Some examples of the types of development that might be appropriate are given in Tables 3a, b and c. These tables show that established frameworks can respond to a changing situation effectively and can, in turn, be strengthened by the new opportunities available.

Guidance phase	Good current practice	Potential on-line additions
Pre-entry guidance	Printed student information Open days Student interviews Educational guidance	Downloadable supplementary information Virtual tours of resources Careers guidance and decision-making materials
Induction	Student handbooks Briefing for library and IT Introduction to subject Student Union introductions Student Services introductions	On-line materials for late entrants, part-time and distance students
Assessment of learning skills/ prior learning	Diagnostic assignment during induction APEL systems or CATS accumulation	On-line self diagnostic tests Subject self tests for module credit APEL on-line using expert system
Assessment of learning and support needs	Diagnostic assessment of basic skills/learning skills available where appropriate	On-line self diagnostic tests to claim support

Table 3a Initial guidance

In developing extended guidance and support frameworks the criteria for success should be borne in mind. Success depends upon:
- consistency in implementing systems so that students have an equivalent experience
- proactive systems – identifying and dealing with problems and issues – rather than reactive (waiting for problems to occur)
- systems being organised coherently to include regular student contact (whether on- or off-line)
- monitoring the effectiveness of implementation to ensure consistency and quality.

Guidance phase	Good current practice	Potential on-line additions
Planning the learning programme	Educational and academic guidance Regular tutorial review	On-line information on pathways and progression E-mail contact with tutors
Assessing, recording and feeding back achievement	Structured formative assessment Feedback on assessment	Self-check subject-related software with consistent feedback Submission of assessment and feedback on-line On-line claiming and recording of, for example, key skills
Formative reviews	Feedback in tutorial review	
Monitoring and tracking student progression	Monitoring and tracking systems to course leader or senior tutor	Use e-mail to log concerns Group spreadsheet to log and identify absences, etc.
Providing learning skills and key skills support	Integrated in programme Integrated in tutor support Skills modules Additional support	On-line activities to develop, assess and record skills Additional workshop materials on-line, e.g. maths packages
Setting expectations and encouraging learning	Through regular academic guidance	

Table 3b Guidance on programme

However successful such adaptations can be, we need to look forward a little to anticipate something of the medium-term future, when the technology will begin to change the shape of delivery more substantially.

Guidance phase	Good current practice	Potential on-line additions
Progression guidance	Educational/careers guidance Integrated careers elements in learning programme Exposure to practitioners in learning programme	Educational/careers information on-line
Summative assessment and recording	Record of achievement	On-line record of achievement

Table 3c Guidance for progression

N.B. With the exception of expert systems for APEL examples of all these on-line additions can be observed in practice in further and higher education, although few are widely adopted.

A medium-term strategy for guidance and support

As on-line provision grows and materials for whole programmes, including teaching, resource and assessment materials are available, the need to assemble students in one place is no longer so necessary. This development is likely to occur first for short and entry level courses – allowing them to be distributed to community learning centres or directly to the home. Whilst computer technology remains expensive and its rapid obsolescence limits its use for those on a lower income, network technology is becoming available through televisions very cheaply, using set-top boxes and net-televisions via cable or phone and digital broadcast. The dominant net-box technology in this country offers a simple and consistent interface which is superior to that used on most PCs. On-line access for all is near to reality. This means that schools, colleges and universities will be able to offer distributed education to their local communities – highly appropriate for many 'lifelong' learners.

The delivery of learning programmes outside institutions could lead to a much greater range of lifelong learning opportunities, run in association with further and higher education, in community and school learning centres. It is likely that the new Learning and Skills Councils will foster such developments.

Support strategies will need to adapt and the principle methods are likely to be:

- on-site technical and front-line academic guidance at the learning centre
- back-up support via e-mail or video-phone to a central programme or learning support tutor
- supplementary guidance materials included as on-line help with learning materials
- separate learning support packages
- self-test and feedback materials in packages
- on-line or off-line academic guidance and tutoring.

In short, a workable scenario will be initial on-line help, with front-line technical and learning support and second-line central support available. This is similar to the strategy being developed by national distributed learning providers and some case studies of their developments are considered in the next chapter.

If the strategy is simply technology driven, we can see

that we fall back to the on-line equivalent of the 'open door' – a reactive, problem fixing strategy, rather than a proactive problem diagnosing and avoidance strategy. This will not meet the needs of students. Evidence *TES (2000)* shows that without adequate frameworks for independent learning – and that means tutoring – many young people regard independent learning time as free period time. Older learners may well find they need considerable support in dealing both with the technology and how manage learning independently.

We will therefore need to include in an appropriate medium-term strategy some way of delivering the proactive monitoring, review and planning elements that enable effective guidance and support provision to develop learning. The key to this may well be the provision of structured tutoring or its equivalent. On-line tutoring will need to implement the elements of the learning development model (refer to Chapter 2) and its integration of teaching, academic guidance and learner support functions.

There are a number of ways this can be delivered:
- regular tutorial slots arranged at learning centres
- the formation of study circles with regular tutorial support at home or work
- the introduction of mentoring for work-based learning
- development of an on-line tutoring facility.

In summary, many of the strategies for the medium-term will resemble those being adopted for distance and distributed learning, which are discussed in the next chapter.

Learning styles On-line learning will not suit all learners. If diversity and choice in education are maintained, substantial numbers of learners will prefer to maintain the computer and the network as useful adjuncts to their learning, not the major means of delivery. Students have different learning styles and not all students will study effectively on-line; others will require considerable initial support to do so.

Meeting the needs of learners is not just limited to providing suitable access to a range of learning programmes with appropriate guidance and support.

The personal circumstances of adult learners and their approach to learning will place different demands on support and different provision strategies.

It is important to recognise that there are also other dimensions which differentiate learners. Honey and Mumford have investigated four learning styles (activist, reflector, theorist, pragmatist) which are combined in various proportions amongst individuals and which give different approaches to learning. Gow and Kember suggest that there is a hierarchy of learning abilities ranging from 'reproduction' to 'strategy':

Honey and Mumford (1986)

Gow and Kember (1993)

- reproduction – the ability to memorise and reproduce material, without necessarily understanding it
- understanding – the ability to learn through understanding and applying material
- strategy – the self-awareness to direct study efficiently and to learn effectively.

Entwhistle (1992)

Understanding and strategic learning promote deep learning against the surface learning promoted by rote and reproduction. A typology of learners by their situation and preferred learning styles is suggested in Table 4. The typology suggests that on-line learning is particularly suited to self-managing learners, and its capacity to be delivered in a wide range of settings – the home, workplace, community or education centre – meets the requirements of people for whom time or distance are barriers. On-line learning will provide an excellent means of delivering work-related and professional development courses into the workplace, particularly on a need-to-know basis. People who need a more social and personal learning environment will continue to seek education in face-to-face settings. In whatever way guidance and support is offered, it should offer a pathway to strategic learning for the learner.

Learner type	Due to circumstance or situation	Due to learning style or preference	Suitable forms of provision
Solo learner	ISOLATED LEARNER Geographical, social or economic isolation e.g.: Shift workers Physical disability NEEDS Flexible provision Integrated support Peer contact	AUTONOMOUS LEARNER High motivation and focus Good learning skills IT literate NEEDS Tracking and monitoring Formative feedback Flexible provision	ISOLATED LEARNER On-line learning programme with integrated on-line support – virtual learning environment AUTONOMOUS LEARNER On-line learning programme with on-line academic guidance
Group learner	TEAM LEARNER Education/training requires team/group skills High social/interactive components in learning programme Development of key skills NEEDS Group or team working Peer contact People interaction	SOCIAL LEARNER Prefers working in groups Enjoys peer contact Profits from discussion NEEDS Personal element to academic guidance Peer support and group working People interaction	TEAM LEARNER On-line learning within a virtual learning environment or traditional off-line provision SOCIAL LEARNER Off-line provision Local/personal academic guidance
Novice learner	ADULT RETURNER Incomplete education – social/family reasons Lacks confidence Improving skills and autonomy NEEDS May need to improve skills Personal academic guidance and support Peer support		ADULT RETURNER Traditional group-based provision or on-line learning in a virtual learning environment Good personal academic guidance and support

Table 4 Learning styles, circumstance and suitable provision

Summary

- The experience of computer-based instruction is that it is an impoverishing method.
- The benefits of computer networks are that they can provide resources for learning.
- The strength of computer networks is that they can hold information efficiently and allow flexible access.
- The new flexibility requires flexible support for learning – which new information technologies make possible.
- Network technologies can augment and enrich good current practice in tutoring.
- As on-line learning is distributed from the institution to the community, support strategies will need to evolve.
- On-line learning will only work for students where learning styles or circumstances favour supported self-study.
- There will be a continuing need for education based on social interaction for many students.

The next chapter looks at some examples of guidance and support practice in distance and distributed learning.

Distance and distributed learning

Distance and distributed learning is an expanding mode of study which is rapidly benefitting from the opportunities offered by network technology. There are well established models of support and guidance on which to draw. The concept of tutoring is central to these and on-line tutoring can be readily integrated into programmes, defining good quality provision.

Not such a new development

In all the excitement about the possibilities of on-line learning and its potential impact on the world of learning, it is easy to forget that we already enjoy a large distance and distributed learning sector, albeit largely paper-based. From crude, and sometimes dishonest, beginnings in the twilight world of correspondence courses, distance learning has emerged as a significant educational route, particularly for lifelong learning. Major organizations such as the National Extension College (NEC), who publish a wide range of materials for use by those delivering open learning, provide many varied niche training opportunities. The market is dominated by the Open University which has by far the largest number of student enrolments of any UK higher education body, and has achieved a creditable record of outcomes in higher education quality assurance visits. The Open University has been phasing in the use of on-line learning for some time in its newly introduced courses, both as an adjunct for its more traditional approaches and as an alternative learning mode. A national e-university is being planned which will draw on existing higher education providers.

Further education also offers a number of well developed provisions. In recent years private training organizations have emerged which offer on-line training environments, although these are largely limited to IT and 'lower level' business training. The FERL website shows a healthy number of further education
www.ferl.co.uk development projects.

A recent entrant into this area is Learndirect – the brand name of the University for Industry (UfI) – which has taken on the challenge of providing a widely used training system for industry and commerce. The UfI's unique selling point is the on-line character of the provision and the availability of learning in short 'bite-sized' chunks.

Learndirect has assumed the challenge addressed in the late 1980s by the Open College. The Open College was established to develop a widely used system of open and distance learning to meet workplace needs. It commissioned a large number of open and distance learning materials and set up a system of learning centres to deliver them, mainly in conjunction with further education colleges. The materials were largely paper-based with little on-line learning. Accredited tutor training courses were set up to enable people to provide guidance and support. It is now recognised that one of the weaknesses of the Open College strategies in the 1980s was its bolt-on guidance and support system. The Open College, rather than selling learning programmes with integrated guidance and support, opted to sell packages with support as a costly extra. The net result was that support was priced out and, without guidance and support built in, the learning packages became less relevant to their purpose.

The Open College became a publisher of distance learning materials subsequently and was sold to a publishing group when the present government set up the UfI. The UfI has attempted to avoid support difficulties and has developed a much more considered approach to guidance and support for Learndirect. Neither the Open College nor the UfI has enjoyed the fundamental advantage of the Open University, which caught the public imagination at a time when there was huge pent up demand from professionally qualified groups, such as teachers and nurses, for graduate status. Learndirect is, however, being heavily promoted on posters and television at the time of writing.

The importance of contemporary developments is that they offer strategies for guidance and support that are already appropriate for their purpose. It is worth comparing the various strategies for support which have been developed and which provide workable frameworks for distance and distributed learning.

The Open University model

www.open.ac.uk/ experience

The Open University has made a large investment in student support and guidance. The key roles are those of tutors and counsellors who are allocated to every student. This system is administered through the 13 regions of the Open University who are responsible for the delivery of services in their region. Four regions have responsibility for students studying outside the UK.

Figure 11 The Open University – a support page

Bailey, Brown and Kelly (1996)

Refer to Table 2 Chapter 2

The approach is to deliver all seven UDACE functions of support and guidance (outlined in Chapter 2) on all aspects of study with the Open University.

The University provides guidance at the pre-entry, entry and on-course stages of a course.

- **Pre-entry guidance** is based on extensive written and on-line material. Prospective students are directed to front-line admissions staff backed up by specialist education guidance workers. An on-line careers diagnostic package is now available to help selection.
- **Entry and induction.** Practice varies according to course and level, but new students are supplied with information packs and those at foundation level are sent preparation packs and can attend introductory meetings. Most courses have an introductory element within them that enables the detection of students who require special support.
- **On-course guidance** is given through a tutorial system that might be conducted via e-mail, telephone, face-to-face, group tutorials or increasingly through virtual learning environments. This is

substantially concerned with students' academic development. Students on undergraduate degree programmes will also have a counsellor who tracks their progress and deals with difficulties. Other guidance – for example, on-course choice – is given regionally. Support for students with disabilities is given centrally.

The Open University provides a limited range of personal guidance, largely concerned with problems relating to time and costs of study, and refers other students to appropriate local guidance services. Guidance for education progression is given as well as information on careers at regional centres.

The Open University maintains a holistic developmental and integrated approach, linking teaching and support roles within tutoring. *'Counselling is seen as an integral part of a student's learning process, grounded in a view of the student as a whole person, whose learning takes place in the* *Fage and Heron* *context of past experiences, present circumstances and future* *(1990)* *hopes and aspirations.'* The level of integration is such *Bailey, Brown and* that *'guidance is often invisible, in the sense it is embedded in* *Kelly (1996)* *the teaching and learning system.'*

The Open University decided in 1998 to move towards greater use of on-line teaching, academic guidance and support. It is increasingly using learning-environment software for its new courses. These provide general discussion areas for students, allow tutor–student discussions and can house additional learning resources on-line. Private tutor contact by e-mail can be accommodated. One advantage of this system is that the course team, who write and manage the course, can be in closer contact with students.

Hennessey, Flude The Open University has conducted some research on *and Tait (1999)* this topic. A survey was carried out over two years with a limited sample of education tutors and students taken from two regions. The survey aimed to be a comprehensive evaluation of academic guidance and support, looking at both the Open University's traditional face-to-face systems and telephone support as well as new electronic systems of conferencing and e-mail support. Principal findings in relation to greater reliance on on-line support were:

- only one-third of students welcomed the greater use

of on-line support
- women were less convinced than men
- older learners (over 44) were less satisfied with on-line tutoring
- costs, time and access were also concerns.

The most highly rated form of support was face-to-face and focussed on assignments, interpreting course materials and examination revision. On the other hand, three-quarters of students and tutors did not use telephone support. The results of this survey may reflect a concern that the development of on-line support might lead to withdrawal of face-to-face guidance. The sample is also not necessarily typical of other learners. Where the Open University students had the choice, however, they preferred face-to-face support.

Organization of guidance and support for Learndirect

The UfI has developed a substantial portfolio of short courses under the Learndirect brand, targeted initially at the business and management, IT, multimedia, retail and distribution sectors. Provision is also made for basic skills learning. Courses are delivered on-line through a network of local learning centres or may be accessed from the home or workplace. All centres provide facilities to choose, purchase and be inducted into the courses. Each course has a defined amount of learning support built in. The UfI recognises the range of support that may be required and intends to take account of

www.learndirect.co.uk learners' needs as well as programme development.

find a course • join us • contact us • about us • login

① learndirect HOME

who can help?

childcare • paying for learning • special needs

- get started
- find a course
- who can help?
- build your business
- get that job

It's all very well to think about learning something new. But what about your other responsibilities?

Such as childcare, for example - so you have peace of mind while you learn? Or paying for learning, if finances are tight and learning's last on your list? And what if a disability makes it difficult for you to contemplate a course?

Click on the underlined words - they'll link you to a solution.

If you need extra help or advice, just ring the **learndirect** helpline. It's free on 0800 100 900. Talk through the issues with our friendly advisors.

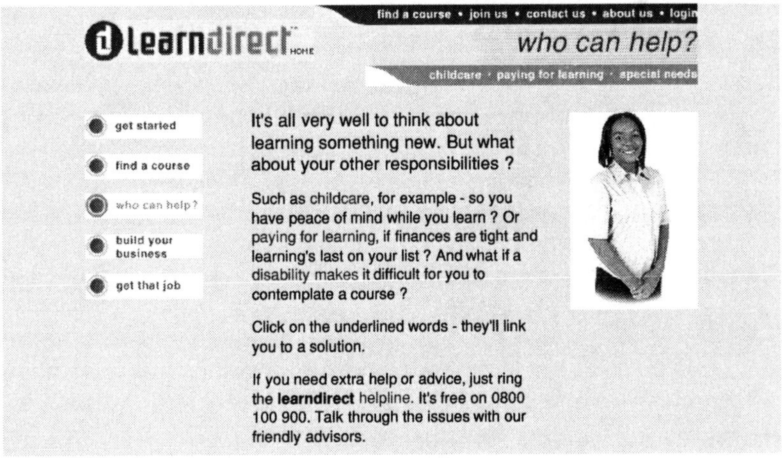

Figure 12 A Learndirect support page

Learndirect exemplifies the integration of guidance and teaching through tutoring. Learning materials are substantially self-contained with on-line or local centre support. Academic guidance is provided on-line through tutoring which may be asynchronous or conducted in realtime. General learning support may be available at the centre. Where provision is made with employers, workplace mentors may be employed.

The UfI stresses the distinctiveness of on-line tutoring and tutoring skills. It believes that these are different from other tutoring skills, that may be practised face-to-face. It offers training in on-line tutoring which covers:

- designing effective on-line learning
- effective implementation and evaluation of on-line learning
- understanding the place of on-line learning within an organization's training strategy
- methods that are available for on-line tutoring
- discussion and development of the range of skills required by on-line tutors.

www.learndirect.co.uk

Support is well organized.

- ***Pre-entry and entry guidance*** are given on-line and through clear publicity materials. Free taster materials on the Learndirect approach and learning skills are given on CD-ROM, with video and workbook support.
- ***On-course*** support is delivered largely through integrated tutoring and technical help is available at the learning centre. Basic skills needs are addressed through specific packages.

At the time of writing, the scope of guidance and support is more limited than for the Open University. The UfI is, however, establishing a dedicated learner services helpline and is promising the learner that they will be *'with you all the way'*.

The e-university Proposals for an e-university are currently being developed. The e-university proposals recognise the need for student guidance and support. They recognise that much support for learning needs to be built into the learning programme but that a range of other support services need to be available. These fall into four categories:

- tutorial support for learning
- assessments, schedules and arrangements
- access to library services and learning facilities
- wider support services.

In their considerations for learning support services, the proposals focus on the use of available and prospective on-line technologies to replicate traditional teaching and learning activities. This essentially envisages a virtual campus type of learning environment that can provide, for example:

- live on-line tutorial
- peer interaction
  - through a mediated web conference or shared whiteboard
  - video-conferencing
  - computer-mediated conferencing using threaded discussions under tutor control
- realtime technical and academic help with a call centre staffed by teaching assistants.

The e-university envisages that specialised tutoring services will be provided on a contracted basis, as in the United States, which could be drawn from higher education or commercial companies. It is also clear that at present much support is seen as an additional cost extra, running the risk of low take-up and a 'bolt-on' support mentality.

There is a risk that the e-university proposals with their emphasis on American experience are likely to emulate the early difficulties experienced by the Open College rather than the continuing success of the Open University.

Support on-line

Both the Open University and Learndirect are showing that on-line guidance and support can be successfully integrated into on-line learning and that a high level of support can be delivered on-line.

The Open University recognises that individual learning needs and learning styles differ and that many learners value a personal link with their tutor. For many, this means a person with whom they can build a face-to-face relationship and who is available either at a learning centre or on a telephone for consultation and advice. The development of broadband communications in the future will allow video-links for realtime, network-based conversations with tutors, so that some aspects of face-to-face communication can be simulated.

For many learners, however, the possibility of face-to-face help and assistance will be an essential requirement for learning. This does not preclude on-line strategies being implemented to deal with front-line enquiries.

Successful on-line provision will offer a form of integrated learning environment. Within this environment there will be areas for teaching materials, assessment and self-assessment activities, tutorial contact and general academic discussion. These can be conducted using a variety of types of communication.

Those which are most important for on-line guidance and support are detailed below. Further information on the implementation of on-line tutoring is given in Chapter 6.

- *Asynchronous communication* is the process of question and response over a period of time that allows reflection. This is particularly useful for students seeking extended comment and is helpful in dealing with questions of understanding course materials and assessment tasks and giving and receiving feedback.
- *Realtime communication*, as, for example, in a chat room or by telephone, is appropriate for peer-to-peer discussion about the course and is useful for tutor intervention in these discussions. It is also helpful for dealing with immediate technical problems and administrative queries.
- In the future, as *broadband communications systems* become more widely available, video-conferencing could allow seminars and discussions to be held with a course tutor, or face-to-face discussion. It is possible that this will allow established patterns of education to persist on networks, with the cost of students' time and travel transferred to high powered network technology.
- *Interactive assessment technologies* are already available. Interesting examples are structured self-tests which give a diagnosis of level achieved, areas for revision or development. Simple testing of knowledge and understanding – for example, through multiple

http://
www.qmark.com

choice questions – can also be carried out, and in some areas skills, such as IT, decision making and simulation can be assessed directly.

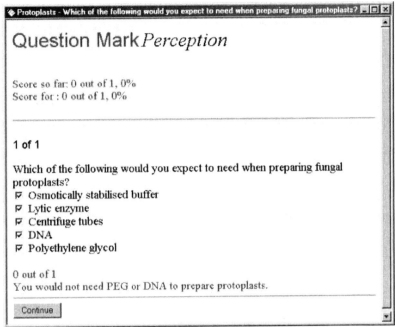

Figure 13 An example of a multiple response question

In on-line learning it is extremely important that assessment is properly designed and supported. The technology should not dictate inappropriate forms of assessment. Instant feedback can be given through self-tests but more developed programmes should offer the opportunity for independent assessment tasks to be completed. These will be generally done off-line, through assignment tasks, or by wordprocessing, with the outcomes e-mailed to a tutor. It is difficult to ensure written feedback is given adequately. Such feedback is extremely important in face-to-face tutoring, but can be supplemented by oral explanation. On-line feedback makes an essential contribution to learning development and therefore it is vital that feedback is consistently well structured, encouraging and full.

The Internet as an educational resource

So far we have looked at structured learning programmes on-line, but perhaps the most impressive aspect of the new communications technologies is the availability of information on-line, through newsgroups, discussion groups and the world wide web. The Internet provides ready access to everyday information from known and reputable sources, news, weather, train times and so on. When we come to learning resources, however, the picture changes.

The problem with any learning resource is to establish its accuracy and authority. There are difficulties with some Internet sources, for example:

Validity – Is this from a reputable source? Does it represent knowledge or opinion? Is it backed up by research or is it unsubstantiated?

Reliability – Is the information provided subject to scholarship? Is it checked and verified?

Coverage – Does the information present a complete or partial view? Is it in-depth or superficial?

The Internet can be a misleading place for unskilled autodidacts. For example, a great deal of the information on offer is weird, inaccurate or simply unreliable. This can seriously mislead inexperienced learners, who have not developed critical equipment. For example, an access student may be interested in the strange phenomena which are documented from time to time – fish or frogs falling as rain, or objects apparently in the sky. Such a student will need to be able to discriminate scaremongering, superstition and conspiracy theorist sources from serious investigation and scientific appraisal. Whilst the former may well have interesting web sites, easily located in search engines, the latter may take place in academic newsgroups, which are deliberately restricted to keep scaremongers, conspiracy theorists and young surfers out.

Some discussion of pitfalls for the uninitiated can be found at www.degree.net

Clearly, skills need to be developed at two levels – Internet search skills and the learning skills of critical appraisal. This means if the Internet is to be used as an educational resource structured guidance and support has to be provided and sometimes controlled.

Skills can be developed directly (if not always easily) through tutorial support in traditional learning programmes or at a learning centre. Since this is an open-ended support commitment, the temptation for distance learning providers is to predigest the range of relevant learning resources or restrict them. On the other hand, the technical skills of, for example, web search for academic purposes and filtering information can be packaged for on-line usage. Whether skills of critical appraisal can be similarly packaged is a more contentious question.

The impact of global communication on learning

The Internet allows the globalisation of knowledge and communication, an important co-requisite of a global economy. There are those optimists who argue that this will inevitably lead to a much greater diversity of information and knowledge that will facilitate a more plural and better educated society.

The pessimists, however, see the Internet sliding towards a domination by multinational corporations. If we consider education as an industry, it is largely in the pre-industrial stage. It offers an enormous choice of handcrafted products, which at adult and higher levels can offer almost a bespoke service to students. Education is about to experience a revolution, brought about by the ability to offer a standard product globally.

www. virtualuniversity.ac provides a portal to many global providers

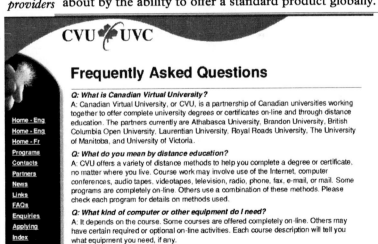

CVU ⚜ UVC

Frequently Asked Questions

Q: What is Canadian Virtual University?
A: Canadian Virtual University, or CVU, is a partnership of Canadian universities working together to offer complete university degrees or certificates on-line and through distance education. The partners currently are Athabasca University, Brandon University, British Columbia Open University, Laurentian University, Royal Roads University, The University of Manitoba, and University of Victoria.

Q: What do you mean by distance education?
A: CVU offers a variety of distance methods to help you complete a degree or certificate, no matter where you live. Course work may involve use of the Internet, computer conferences, audio tapes, videotapes, television, radio, phone, fax, e-mail, or mail. Some programs are completely on-line. Others use a combination of these methods. Please check each program for details on methods used.

Q: What kind of computer or other equipment do I need?
A: It depends on the course. Some courses are offered completely on-line. Others may have certain required or optional on-line activities. Each course description will tell you what equipment you need, if any.

Home - Eng
Home - Eng
Home - Fr
Programs
Contacts
Partners
News
Links
FAQs
Enquiries
Applying
Index

Figure 14 Canadian Virtual University

Corporations are gearing up to produce on-line materials and writing teams are being assembled. Henceforth, colleges and universities will be faced with competition from highly developed educational products, which can be purchased on-line. Given the investment which is being made, these products will be slick and, at one level at least, they will be well written, because capable and experienced writers are being recruited to undertake the work. As a result education will become, another commodity to be bought and sold, rather than a social right which we have hitherto (although decreasingly) understood it to be.

What is more, it is a commodity which, despite the investment, could be offered more cheaply than institutional-based education, by concentrating simply on teaching and assessment. The pressure by higher education for higher fees, allied with the debt burden of the study period, could pose enormous threats to traditional further and higher education.

The plus side of this development is that it could enable much broader access to education. Materials are likely to be extremely well organised and presented and contain high quality content. It is almost certain that universities which find themselves under economic pressure will be prepared to validate and accredit the provision. The downside is that it may return education to the level of sophistication of an 'old style' correspondence course. The logic of consumption is that you gain satisfaction by buying and owning a product, not necessarily by using it. High attrition rates will be normal, reversing the values of education seen as a public good which places a premium on completion and achievement.

This can, of course, be countered if corporations invest in guidance and support, creating local learning centres, which they could do easily in partnership with schools and colleges. The experience of the late 1980s in arranging support for Open College courses is, however, that the public were unwilling to pay the considerable on-costs of support, compared to the low package purchase price.

There is, however, a further consideration. In a globalised provision of education, even if tailored to local markets, how much diversity is likely to be present? It is possible that some of the new provisions will have a liberal educational agenda, but how can this reflect the vast range of knowledge production in, for example, the social sciences? If we enter a period of global mass education, however well produced, the validity of the courses, or the liberal stance of its provision, the fact remains that each course unit will be highly focused and directed and draw upon a limited range of references. At least one provider is envisaging using broadband technology to place lectures on the web, an endeavour, it must be said, of dubious educational worth because it replicates an outdated and inappropriate model for on-line learning.

There is a real danger here. Suppose that a major global education corporation provides courses in economics. They may reflect a particular economic orthodoxy which underlies the corporate viewpoint and excludes critical views. If diversity of provision is diminished, the economic basis to sustain critical scholarship is lessened. The academic landscape would then effectively experience enclosure by corporations who may fence in or even attempt to own ideas. Ideological hegemony will accompany economic domination, with grave consequences for plural democracy.

It is therefore essential that diversity in educational thought is sustained. This will require education providers to adapt the new possibilities of on-line learning, whilst ensuring that they are capable of developing critical ability in their students. In conventional learning programmes this requires the teaching, guidance and support skills which we have identified as tutoring, and, however it is delivered, tutoring is likely to be integral to any liberal educational offer.

Summary

- There is a long history of distance and open learning which provides a context for current on-line developments.
- Earlier experiences in developing distributed learning show the importance of integrating guidance and support.
- The Open University has a well developed support structure which is adapting to the introduction of on-line learning.
- The UfI through Learndirect is attempting to set up a support structure from first principles.
- On-line tutoring is a central activity in all current developments and the techniques of on-line tutoring are central to the provision of support.
- The world wide web provides a huge educational resource, but requires skilled use and interpretation for learning purposes.
- We are seeing the beginnings of the globalization of learning. This offers wider access but also may threaten liberal conceptions of education.
- Guidance and support systems are integral if liberal approaches are to be maintained.

The next chapter considers the delivery of support and guidance at the pre-entry and entry stage.

Initial guidance, selection and diagnostic assessment

Initial guidance helps students to make the right choice of learning programme and providers to retain students 'on-course'. Diagnostic assessment can assist this process, in appropriate circumstances. There is much that can be offered on-line, but some work is more appropriately delivered face-to-face.

The role of initial guidance Chapter 2 introduced the importance of guidance and support to student retention and completion and emphasised its role in relation to contemporary approaches to teaching and learning. It then distinguished various types of guidance which it is desirable to develop to ensure that students remain on-programme and enjoy successful learning experiences.

Initial guidance is involved at the stage at which students make their choice of programme. The range of choice involves not just the subject of study (nursing or engineering) but also the type of qualification (G/NVQ, A-level or Access) the level of study (diploma, degree or postgraduate) and the mode of study (taught, distance or on-line). In addition, the potential student may want to know about the quality of provision, the level of student success and achievement or the ethos and approach to learning.

Every student has different expectations and requirements, many of which go beyond the learning programme. If all the circumstances are not right, the motivation to study will be reduced.

The most commonly given reasons for withdrawal from study are problems of finance, relationships, childcare and housing. Well organised guidance and support can do much to help students deal with *Hall and Corney* problems and remain on-programme. A study carried *(1995)* out in the mid 1990s suggests, however, that many students who successfully complete their studies experience these problems with equal severity to those who drop out. Students withdraw and fail even in the most supportive environments. The most likely causes are that they are unhappy, unmotivated, or that they are studying the wrong subject or at the wrong level. These reasons do not emerge as reasons for leaving because students find it easier to displace their difficulties into areas which are less threatening to their own (or their teacher's) self-image.

The best way to deal with such problems is to ensure that students make fully informed choices about what and how they study. The problem is that they do not have perfect information. They face the problem most people face when choosing a mobile phone or making a financial investment, which is having:

- a confusing range of choices
- a plethora of incompatible information
- great difficulty identifying the most relevant information
- difficulty locating informed and impartial advice.

In such circumstances choices are often made based on irrelevant information or as a result of partial and self-interested advice. Quite frequently mistakes are made. Good initial guidance is therefore the foundation upon which the student and the provider can build success.

Factors in student choice of programme

There is a wide range of choices that are involved when a person selects an education programme, although few people actually start with a totally open set of possibilities. There will almost certainly be a number of limitations which restrict choice and a set of preferences or avoidances within the range of choices available.

Most learners will experience a number of constraints and so will make choices that are based on these limits. Typical considerations might be:

- When can I study?
- Where can I study?
- What does it cost?

In addition to these questions, learners may have strong preferences and avoidances about the type of provision they undertake. Despite the very wide range of educational approaches which were tried out during the last century, many people from all age groups left school lacking confidence in their educational abilities or with a dislike of the school approach. Equally, many older learners are wary of new technology. There are many barriers to access which simply reflect people's pre-conceptions about learning, or their lack of confidence in skills which they may later find they can easily acquire. Many entrants will need to be reassured of their potential to make the most of the opportunities that are available. People who are returning to education for work or self-improvement reasons often have little concept of the scope and variety of education or the range of choice available. Nor do they have well developed criteria to assess the suitability of provision they are offered.

More experienced or self-confident learners will want to make advanced choices about the appropriateness of provision. Sophisticated learners may have a strong preference for particular styles of delivery and assessment – for example, wanting provision with good opportunities for practical application and assessment by assignments (showing the ability to apply knowledge and understanding) rather than examinations.

If learners are contemplating provision where on-line learning is a major component, whether this is workplace training, a distance learning programme or within a community setting, they are likely to want to work through a list of information requirements which at minimum will cover:

- the programme(s) offered, the appropriateness of those programmes to perceived educational and career needs
- the type and currency of any qualification offered, the costs of study and any likely financial support from employers, providers or government
- the times at which study opportunity is available, in work time, in the evenings or flexibly
- the means of access to on-line study – through a home-based computer or through a learning centre, at work, in the community, or at a providing institution – and the time and financial costs of access
- the quality and reputation of the provider, the design and quality of on-line and paper-based learning materials, any kite-marking that is applicable
- on-line or off-line teaching and tutoring provided with the programme
- technical and academic support available, when and how (by e-mail, phone link, on-line video-link)

- the type, form and purpose of assessment, whether on- or off-line arrangements for self-testing, feedback. Over and above this range of information, potential learners are likely to need to understand the differences with an on-line approach to learning, and to appreciate whether this is suitable for their particular learning needs and styles.

Providing initial guidance

All students need good quality information and many need additional help with understanding the options that are available and selecting the most appropriate one. Some will require in-depth guidance to help them determine what their real needs are, and in which directions they are most likely to succeed. There are a number of stages of initial guidance, which include:
- pre-entry guidance
- preliminary information
- guidance and selection for entry
- guidance and induction on entry.

These stages within the guidance model have a close correspondence with what in marketing jargon is called 'customer orientation' which entails:

Hatton and Sedgemoor (1992)

- communicating information effectively
- identifying needs and finding better ways of meeting them
- helping people to make informed choices.

Appropriate initial guidance is therefore a part of an effective marketing and recruitment strategy that builds customer confidence, satisfaction and retention.

Pre-entry guidance

The field of pre-entry guidance is somewhat competitive and there are a large number of potential sources of information.

- ***Generic information and guidance*** is provided by education and careers advisory services contracted by local Learning and Skills Councils. Such services cater for a wide range of clients including school leavers, adult returners and ex-offenders. These services have a good overview of the whole range of provision and providers, and can give the specialist diagnostic help that enables people to make significant changes of direction in their education and training. For an individual wanting to discuss the merits of a wide range of educational possibilities, supported by comprehensive information and appropriate diagnostic tests these services are a very good way to gain an overview of the options.

- *The Department of Employment* and its contractors also offer some degree of guidance to long term unemployed people. This is fairly elementary and is often strongly geared to particular programmes such as New Deal which the government of the day is offering. Nevertheless, such services do often give considerable support for individuals and enable them to take the first successful steps in lifelong education.

- *Many colleges and universities* also give guidance, which might range from a full guidance and information service, to help and advice on the particular programmes and modes offered by the institution. Whilst such services generally do not claim the same degree of impartiality as education guidance providers, they are able to offer sensible and professional advice which is geared to helping students who have a reasonably clear notion of their own constraints and preferences, find a closely matching provision.

- There has been considerable experimentation with the provision of educational guidance on-line, with mixed results. Watts (1995) gives a summary of the issues which concludes that current technology *'may presage the transition to the third age of computer aided guidance systems . . . a period in which the locus of control in the usage of such systems – which in the first period belongs to the system, and in the second to the interactive interface between the system and the individual – passes to a much more significant extent to the individual.'*

Watts (1995)

An attractive option for on-line providers is to attempt to offer on-line guidance, for example, on a web site. Once beyond the basic information stage, this starts to become a time- and resource-consuming activity. The Open University does, however, have an effective downloadable package. Most providers find it simpler to refer to established guidance services who can be primed to offer appropriate guidance. Most often this will be the education and careers guidance provider, a college or university guidance service or a guidance session at a community learning centre. Until such time as self-evident and user-friendly expert systems are devised for impartial and comprehensive guidance, and the huge task of data collection and analysis is resourced, full on-line guidance is unlikely to develop. The next few years will undoubtedly demonstrate some neat but provider-specific innovations in this field.

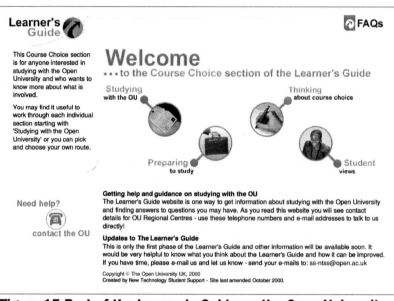

Figure 15 Part of the Learner's Guide on the Open University web site

Preliminary information

This is one area where a huge transfer from paper-based to electronically held information is taking place. Preliminary information about a programme, content, study requirements, time commitments, teaching and learning materials and assessment requirements can answer a large number of the preference questions that a potential learner will need. Almost all this information can be attractively presented on a web site and also put in downloadable form, making it much more widely and easily available, and cost-effectively distributed.

Figure 16 A higher education web site – showing the range of information available

www.chelt.ac.uk To be most useful such information should give a rounded picture. Those people who are unlikely to find the mode of study, programme content or learning requirements suitable should be able to identify this quickly, rather than withdrawing at a later stage, thus wasting their time and resources.

Guidance and selection for entry
In the past, recruitment for further education generally took place by students simply arriving at an enrolment event, and for higher education through the clearing house (such as UCAS) based upon predicted and actual A-level grades. Whilst such systems are easy to administer, they do not necessarily promote the 'best fit' between the needs and the qualities of the student and the nature and expectations of the programme. Best practice now gives more information to students and provides a careful interview so that students and education providers can ensure that the programme is appropriate.

Education providers will want to identify students in

more competitive situations who will benefit most from the type of education offered, or in less competitive situations who are likely to succeed. Where open access policies are operating, it is particularly important that students are helped to enter at an appropriate level, and that they know the demands that are made and the support available to meet them. Some providers use selection tests to identify such students, but the appropriate use of indicators in guidance interviews has a good success rate, without the disadvantages of testing. Appropriate uses from diagnostic assessments are discussed later in this chapter.

Hurley, Smith and Hurley (1995)

This is clearly a crucial stage in the guidance process. Whilst institutionally based providers of on-line learning may be able to offer some highly developed systems for personal entry guidance and selection, it is difficult for distance learning providers to offer the same facilities. One consequence is that, in general, withdrawal from such programmes is around twice the rate of similar conventional programmes.

This is a problem if, as predicted, distributed on-line learning becomes a major form of provision. We may need to rethink some of the preconceptions about how guidance is provided, to retain the personal link. For example, if on-line learning becomes a significant element in workplace training in major companies as predicted, then it follows that company human resource development strategies may need to include appropriate guidance and support for on-line learning, from appropriately trained personnel. If community access develops as predicted, then some guidance functions will need to be located at the community learning centre. What is difficult to avoid at some stage is the personal contact upon which mutual confidence is built. The development of wider bandwidth telecommunications which allow simultaneous video-links with computer interaction may allow such activity to be conducted at a distance.

IT Training (1999)

Guidance and induction on entry

Students are generally given all the information that pertains to their learning programme prior to entry on to a course. This may include the objectives of the programme, the content, teaching activities, learning materials, assessment criteria, assessment tasks, arrangements for academic guidance and feedback on assessment. This is normally provided in paper form, but is easily adapted for on-line access whatever the dominant mode of delivery.

Induction gives an important opportunity to the learner to understand the purposes and outcomes of the programme, the resources available and all relevant matters affecting the learning process. This might be a week for a long programme or a few minutes of introduction to a short on-line package.

Induction will include further information that is essential to the learner, such as how to use the information technology effectively or access academic and technical support via e-mail. This is particularly important where more complex systems and software are being used.

There is no difficulty in providing induction activities on-line. They will require careful design and close monitoring by academic staff, but a student-managed on-line induction pack is entirely feasible. Such a pack will contain at the minimum:

- an introduction to/tutorial on the software and communications technology being used in the programme, and information on technical support
- standard student information about the programme structure, contents and assessment
- information about tutor guidance, support and feedback on- or off-line and any specific additional support available at a learning centre or workplace
- a database of learning resources with live links to allow them to be accessed/ordered/downloaded
- any supporting materials such as initial self-tests, glossaries, research indexes, or helpful web sites which assist the student's initial comprehension of the programme content.

Initial diagnostic assessment All learning programmes require a certain level of knowledge and skill if they are to be completed successfully. This includes key skills such as numeracy, and at a higher level analytical ability, and subject-specific skills. In traditional programmes a common activity during induction is to set a simple assignment task which requires a number of relevant key skills to be demonstrated and which introduces students to the demands of the programme. This is an excellent way of making an initial diagnosis of learning needs in relation to the programme and helping the student understand the demands of learning.

If on-line learning is being provided as part of the educational mix on a conventional programme, IT usage and information retrieval can simply be incorporated in a diagnostic assignment. If on-line learning is the main delivery mechanism, we need to consider some further factors.

Demands of the learning programme
All programmes have a defined threshold, what they assume in terms of knowledge, key and subject skills and defined outcomes. Both the level of threshold and the gradient of difficulty may vary.

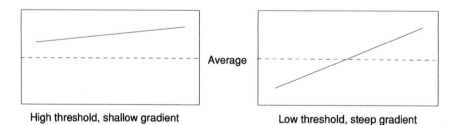

High threshold, shallow gradient
Average
Low threshold, steep gradient

Figure 17a Gradient of difficulty

A programme with a low threshold and a reasonably steep gradient would be described as accessible and challenging (generally regarded as good characteristics); one with a high threshold and shallow gradient would be considered selective and undemanding.

The gradient of difficulty may not be uniformly steep. If it becomes more difficult towards the end of a programme, it helps to differentiate achievement, whilst enabling all learners to benefit. This is the ideal learning curve. If the main difficulties are front-loaded, however, learners may hit a brick wall.

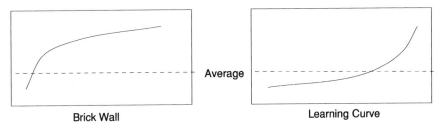

Brick Wall   Learning Curve

Figure 17b The learning curve

One problem for on-line learning is that due to the design of common operating systems (instanced in Chapter 3), many people, both young and old, find great difficulty with initial understanding. This difficulty is repeated for each new software package. This is why the first step in support for on-line learning is to consider the design of the package and integrate support within it.

Learners' needs
Once we have developed packages with accessible thresholds and well structured, demanding learning curves we can consider learners' needs.

Not all learners on any programme will have identical skills and needs. Someone with good A-level achievements may have a number of skills in dealing with assignments and examinations. An adult returner may be able to relate concepts to their experience in a sophisticated and creative way. If both enter a programme at undergraduate level, one may have difficulties organising their studies, the other organising their life. These difficulties will depend on the person and their situation.

In the same way each student will bring a set of key and subject skills to their programme. In some areas these may be well above the threshold for the programme, but in others the relevant key or subject skills may need to be acquired. Some of these skills may be taught or developed explicitly (or less desirably implicitly) in the programme, but some may need additional tutoring to ensure that the student can tackle all aspects of the task. These areas are best discovered early.

One way to identify any mismatch between learners' existing skills, the demands of programmes and any subsequent support needs is to undertake some form of diagnostic assessment or self-assessment.

Diagnosing support needs
Bartram (1999)

On-line assessment of learning needs and learning potential has been piloted in a joint development project by FEDA and Hull University. The project explored approaches to initial assessment and concluded that most materials used were untrialed, non-transferable, arbitrary and confusing. They also tend to relate to past experience rather than future success. The national project set out to provide a set of standardised on-line tools for assessment, based on an established psychological framework for abilities. A number of computer-based tests were developed to key skills specifications, which are being promoted as guides to both ability and support needs. The tests are also being designed to measure personal skills, interests, motivation and personal style.

Test batteries provide a powerful learning needs assessment tool, but there are considerable doubts in theory and in practice about whether these are the best way of determining these needs. Setting a battery of formal computer tests is a formidable disincentive to students, many of whom are well able to cope with the demands of learning. Such tests also tend to be self-confirming as students who do not do well in them are often weeded out of provision. This raises questions about student access to programmes which challenge and extend their abilities.

The DfEE key skills web site offers an overview of the diagnostic testing tools that are available and some criteria for their evaluation.

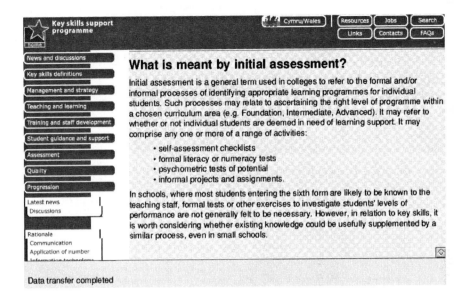

Figure 18 DfEE key skills and initial assessment

www. A recommended approach to diagnosing support
keyskillssupport.net needs in on-line provision is therefore:

- to ensure that pre-entry guidance includes information on the course demands
- to provide a simple self-test to diagnose support needs, directly related to the programme (for short programmes)
- to provide an initial diagnostic assessment activity (for longer programmes)
- to have a help desk available which can log support needs
- to have diagnostic test batteries available as a guidance resource, for use in particular cases where other indications suggest these are appropriate.

Summary

- Students have partial knowledge and information on which to make choices about study.
- Good initial guidance should aim to enable students to find the appropriate programme given their personal needs and constraints.
- There is a wide range of pre-entry guidance of variable quality – the provision of on-line guidance has had mixed success.
- The web is highly suited to providing student information, both pre-entry and at induction.
- Some guidance functions will continue to rely on face-to-face contact, particularly where wider opportunities or inclusive entry are sought.
- Initial assessment is often necessary to ensure that the demands of a learning programme and the learner's threshold skills and learning needs are appropriately balanced.
- Careful diagnosis of support needs may be necessary, in consequence.
- Diagnostic testing should be appropriate to the programme and the level of support need.

The next chapter considers academic guidance and tutoring on-course.

Providing academic guidance and tutorial support for on-line learning

Tutoring should be an integral part of on-line learning programmes both as a teaching tool and as a mechanism for guidance and support. This chapter will consider the requirements for learning development through the programme and then consider what this may mean for the organization of tutoring or mentoring roles. The scope of tutoring for learning development and its delivery on-line are discussed.

An integrated approach

As we look at the way that on-line learning is developing we can see that it is offering two strategic opportunities. The first is to enrich traditional learning programmes, by providing a substantial resource and information base on-line. The second is to create a learning environment. Learning environments can be developed for institutional resource-based learning, distributed learning (with a local centre) or for on-line (possibly global) distance learning.

This book has argued that providing learning environments entails an important set of consequences for teaching, learning and academic guidance. Whilst it is possible to provide just teaching and assessment materials on-line, this is not likely to promote learning effectively. Indeed, it reverts to the older syllabus and exam concept mentioned in Chapter 1. What is required to exploit the full potential of on-line learning is guidance and support to help students learn. An effective on-line learning programme will include tutoring which links elements of teaching, academic guidance and support. Tutoring will be more effective if it is seen as integral to the learning, rather than an afterthought bolted on to deal with problems.

Refer to Chapter 2

The nature of on-line learning tends towards a learner development model of tutoring because it uses guidance to promote learning. As we have already noted, however, whilst elements of this can easily be delivered on-line, there are elements that may require a personal link and possibly face-to face contact. Finding the right balance between what can routinely be delivered on-line and what requires some additional strategies is an important part of the initial programme design.

The nature of the programme will also determine the support requirements. A short, five-hour programme delivered at a learning centre may require only very general support available at the learning centre, call centre or on-line. A long and demanding programme needs more sustained support and for these programmes a nominated tutor or a nominated workplace mentor may be necessary.

Planning the learning programme The requirements of a learning programme can be seen from two points of view, that of the provider and that of the learner.

From the provider's point of view, it is important to ensure the coherence of students' experience and to enable them to achieve the identified learning outcomes. A good learning programme will not only include well designed teaching materials, activities and resources to facilitate learning and assessment tasks which consolidate learning and measure achievement. It will also integrate a number of guidance and support functions.

The essential elements that a provider will need to make available are given in Table 5.

Information	about the aims and outcomes of the programme, content, learning activities, assessment requirements and outcomes, assessment criteria.
Help	through guidance and support systems – ranging from immediate technical help to tutoring.
Opportunity for reflection and learner development	through feedback on assessment tasks and, on longer programmes, structured opportunities to review and plan learning.

Table 5 The essential elements that a provider will need to make available in a good learning programme

From a learner's point of view a somewhat similar list of requirements is apparent. The first requirement is again information, although the range of information may be more substantial than is necessary just to construct a coherent programme. Learners seeking to plan a programme of education will need:

• initial educational guidance on programme choice, including the range that is available, information on the content, learning activities, assessment and outcomes of each one, the time and commitment to study and questions about the place and mode of delivery (home, learning centre, etc.)

- related information that influences access, costs (and financial support), available technical support, academic guidance, support for particular needs (e.g. overcoming disabling barriers or learning difficulties)
- information needed for planning – particularly whether study can be self-paced or is subject to deadlines.

Learners may also need help at the commencement of a programme to assist them to organise themselves for study. This could be handled in an induction package for longer programmes. They will certainly need to learn or have acquired:

- the technical skills to access the network and use the learning environment; this may trigger a need for initial technical support
- the learning skills to tackle study systematically and (on longer programmes) to schedule their work patterns, study and assessment activities; this may trigger the need for immediate tutorial contact and support.

Opportunities for reflection and learning development are likely to manifest themselves for the learner at the planning stage, in questions about significant unknowns – what is expected, how demanding will it be, what depth of study is required? Some of these could be handled in the form of a frequently asked questions (FAQ) sheet, although many people find these boring and off-putting. Tutorial support for reflecting on and planning learning is therefore more desirable.

In longer and more demanding programmes learners need to understand expectations, manage their workload and motivation, schedule on-line and off-line tasks and give themselves opportunities to review and organise learning. It is unhelpful to prescribe these activities, because it disables learner autonomy. Such tasks in any self-managed learning system need to be negotiated *For information on* between the learner and tutor and so initial tutor/learner *negotiation skills refer* guidance is an essential requirement for longer *to Chapter 7* programmes. Whether this is face-to-face, live on-line or by telephone, it requires both personal contact and a degree of interactivity to complete the negotiations.

In such negotiations the aim is to build up the capacity of learners to reflect on the demands of the learning programme, their own approaches to learning and to develop a schedule and an action plan that recognises the constraints on their learning (such as work and family commitments) but gives them the time, space and opportunity to learn effectively. Tutors in personal contact at this stage can:

- set expectations
- motivate students through encouragement and by helping them to solve problems
- help students plan and self-manage their learning
- encourage self-reflection about learning.

This requires some form of realtime communication. It is a much more tortuous process through asynchronous communication.

Strategies for tutoring achievement and managing learning In longer programmes initial tutorial contact should establish an effective tutorial relationship which can include both teaching and guidance tasks. Strategies for shorter programmes may differ and will be discussed below. On longer programmes tutoring will incorporate teaching functions that help learners to:

- understand the content of the learning programme
- undertake activities and assessment tasks
- develop the skills and strategies the learner employs to carry out tasks.

The tutor will also carry out an academic guidance role by:

- dealing with choices
- reviewing achievement and planning strategies for study
- developing the skills and strategies for learner self-management.

The tutor will need to agree with the learner any structures for reviewing progress and achievement, if these are not prescribed by the programme. The activities through which the tutor can help the student to achieve success and the management tasks required are discussed below.

On shorter programmes teaching and guidance functions are still linked, but the requirements of the programme are likely to be more highly prescribed. The time pressures on these programmes also mean that learners will be more willing to trade off speed of response for the personal link. A response from the duty tutor at a learning centre, or the tutor on-line at a help desk, at that particular moment, may be what is required for questions about understanding, process or technical demands. What is more important here is good record keeping systems and the consistency of advice. Record systems should show precisely what previous help and advice has been given. Consistency and quality are necessary for all on-line tutoring, but are essential for tutoring short on-line programmes, if a corporate tutoring rather than individual tutor strategy is chosen.

Developing learning Tutors share responsibility with their students to develop and manage learning. As learners become more independent their ability to self-manage is paramount. This ability has to be developed and learners at an earlier stage in their learning skills will need considerable direction and management. Managing learning requires a number of activities which involve variously teaching, guidance and support.

Tutoring on line
In Chapter 4 the principle means of communications on-line were briefly introduced. The two principal types are asynchronous communications and realtime (synchronous) communications.

Asynchronous communication has been described as an '*on-line Socratic dialogue*', which captures perfectly the sense of discussion over time. There are many forms of asynchronous communication which include e-mails, newsgroups, discussion webs and bulletin boards. Such communications have several advantages.
- They give time for reflection and for participants to compose a considered contribution.
- They provide a record of discussions which can be used subsequently.
- They allow contributions to be made over a period of

time – particularly useful if participants are in different time zones or work shifts.

The most widely encountered form of asynchronous discussion is e-mail. In addition to the other advantages, e-mail can give the assurance that the recipient will get the message (and even provide an acknowledgement) and is likely to yield a reasonably quick response.

Clive Shepherd gives some useful tips for managing e-mail:

- check daily but not too often
- respond quickly, even if it is only an acknowledgement, but better to respond right away so you don't have to duplicate effort
- forward mail to be attended to by someone else, or to your new location, while you are away
- file important messages in a systematic way
- make the header meaningful
- put the main points at the beginning
- keep paragraphs short, use plain English and be concise (but not abrupt)
- use attachments only for big documents.

(www.fastrack-consulting.co.uk)

Like any other form of student discussion, on-line discussion groups need to be managed by the tutor. This is helped by:

- a clear set of rules for use of the discussion group and behaviour within it
- clear objectives and boundaries for the scope of the discussion
- some starting points, which initiate discussion
- encouragement to students to start their own points for discussion.

Tutors will need to stop discussions straying off course by directing them back to the main point, or by summarising and closing a discussion, if it is exhausted. Tutors will also need to enforce the rules, if necessary. If an individual has broken the rules, this is best dealt with outside the discussion group by, for example, sending a private e-mail or making a telephone call.

Realtime (synchronous) communication on-line includes chat rooms, electronic whiteboards and video-conferencing. Realtime communications are useful when all the participants can be together at the same time and instant responses are required. This is useful for checking that each member of a group has received information or understood an analytical construct.

Once more, realtime communications will need to be managed by the tutor. This will be helped by:

- rules of communication, such as how to make a contribution
- clear goals and a limited time frame
- policies on whether private discussions are useful or allowable – as they would be if students were being asked to work in pairs and report back.

The tutor's role is to keep discussion on track – as they would in a seminar. A number of familiar seminar techniques are relevant.

- To encourage contributions, ask questions to which everyone must respond, or direct questions specifically to quieter participants – drawing other participants in helps to manage more dominant contributors.
- Keep the discussion on course by summarising and by posing new questions/discussion points which move the discussion forward, or redirect it to a central issue which remains unresolved.
- Maintain group co-operation and discipline.

Realtime discussion can also be useful for one-to-one tutoring especially using an electronic whiteboard where diagrams, drawings, graphs, etc., can be produced and discussed, or when an application is being shared.

The role of assessment

Assessment has a critical contribution to make to developing learning. The purpose of assessment is not just to test the achievement of learning outcomes but is also to consolidate and develop learning through assessed activities.

There is a temptation in designing on-line programmes to use only forms of assessment such as multiple choice tests, which can be computer marked.

On-line assessment certainly has a place and is particularly useful for:

- allowing learners to self-check their acquisition of knowledge
- stage tests which allow learners to progress through elements of a programme
- summative testing of knowledge acquisition.

There is a range of on-line assessment techniques. Figure 19 shows some of the techniques available on one software package, Question Mark. The advantage of such software is that it can give instant feedback, helping the learner to develop their knowledge base.

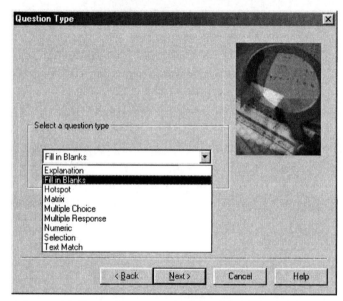

Figure 19 Techniques that are available for assessment in Question Mark Perception

Guardian 19.9.00   Research in the United States, however, where on-line assessment is widely used, suggests that it contributes relatively little to developing understanding or skills. Whereas IT and numerical skills can be directly assessed on-line, communication skills cannot always be assessed so immediately. On-line assessment may be ideal for short knowledge-based materials, or where skills can be simulated. Any longer accredited programme is likely to involve a wider range of assessment activities which are more demanding of learners and may need extended periods of off-line activity.

An important function of tutoring is therefore to enable students to develop their learning through assessment. In part this may involve on-line or personal discussion of tasks, requirements and approaches. There is also much merit in peer discussion in a virtual coffee bar (chat room). Many learning environments make a place available so that students can discuss the programme and share experiences. In one example, in a technical subject, a student noticed an ambiguity in a question and in asking other students to share their interpretation alerted the course tutor to a problem which was clarified, in realtime to the students involved and to all students by e-mail. Quite clearly it is also helpful for students to have direct recourse to a tutor to deal with such issues.

Assessment also produces essential material for the guidance process. It allows a check to be made on student progress, for student tracking and monitoring purposes and formative review and action planning. It enables tutoring to be directed at areas where the learner requires guidance and support. It provides evidence for feedback to the learner of the development of their skills. The integration of assessment and guidance is therefore essential.

Recording, tracking and monitoring

Most systems of on-line provision have software to track on-line events, such as logging on, time spent on-line or activities undertaken. This information is useful as far as it goes – rather like a class register. To make use of it requires some proactive monitoring – checking whether the learner is logging on and progressing through the material and contacting students to talk through any problems.

Alongside this, there is a need to judge the students' level of understanding and skills acquisition. Staged self-tests and formative assessment can provide information that can be recorded and tracked. This provides data, not just to show that the student is progressing but how well they are achieving the learning objectives, which can be monitored and used as a basis for proactive tutoring.

Learning management systems are available which provide most of the necessary facilities.

- On-line systems for tracking usage and monitoring progress – for example, the FIND system in use by Abacus training – are widely available.
- Virtual campus learning environment software may also provide facilities to track student usage and monitor progress.

However tutoring is delivered, a live student tutorial record needs to be maintained which ideally brings all these sources of information together and provides a firm basis for academic guidance. This is especially true if the tutorial support is on-line. In all cases records need to be kept of tutorial guidance to help maintain consistency.

www.abacustraining .co.uk

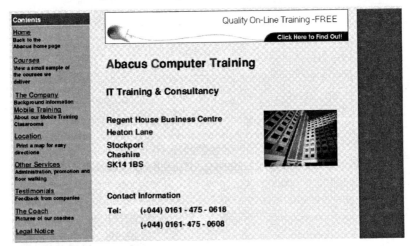

Figure 20 Abacus homepage

Feedback to the learner

Giving feedback on their performance is an essential part of helping students to learn. From well constructed feedback, learners can find where they met the assessment criteria, how well they met these criteria and what they need to do to improve their performance. Feedback is an essential element in developing learning skills (organisational, analytical, critical and research skills) and a key function in academic guidance.

As many higher education subject quality reports show, getting consistency in feedback to students is not easy. If we remove face-to-face communication and the oral channel, however, it becomes even more essential that written feedback is consistently full, relevant and developmental.

What we may conclude from this is that:

- we may wish to include the possibility of face-to-face or oral communication within the academic guidance systems – delivered via learning centre tutors, by web cameras or telephone
- the quality of written feedback is central to the process of on-line tutoring.

Written feedback is usually best delivered through asynchronous communication (for example, via e-mail or equivalent in a learning environment), since reflection is essential to both the giving and receiving of feedback. Feedback should be carefully structured under headings, with topics the tutor may need to comment on under each heading and an opportunity for more holistic comment to develop general themes. Obviously this structure will change with the complexity of the task, its level of ambition and the particular learning outcomes, to which feedback should be matched. For longer, higher level programmes, feedback may therefore be an extended commitment for the tutor.

Feedback should be made available in a standard format. Best practice would suggest that a student should have the opportunity to respond to the feedback and indicate any personal actions/objectives they wish to achieve, before returning the feedback for 'filing'. Students and tutors may wish to review the achievement of these actions at a later date.

There are some circumstances where instantaneous feedback may be more appropriate. This is particularly so where the learner is undertaking short self-tests, or stage tests which are monitoring the acquisition of knowledge, understanding or skills. Here instant on-line feedback can be programmed into the test and suggestions given on any work that could be redone together with suggestions on supplementary learning materials or where to progress. This is a very useful possibility that can be embedded in software, but any system which is totally reliant on computer-generated feedback will be inadequately developmental. It is possible that expert systems will, in future, be able to replicate diagnosis and feedback on learning needs, but expert systems generally provide only a guide to professional decisions, not a substitute for them.

Review and action planning
In addition to feedback on assessment, in longer programmes it is advisable to build in opportunities for periodic review during, or at the end of, the learning programme. This may or may not be a mandatory part of the programme. Certainly, a proactive tutorial review is essential to support students who are in difficulty. Whether review is optional or mandatory for other students will depend on the nature and level of the programme.

Relatively little existing further vocational education on-line, whether through colleges or private trainers, incorporates structured tutorial review, even though this is an essential part of the learner development model of tutoring. Longer programmes will certainly need some form of periodic review. Tutorial review considers:
- progress through the programme and achievement
- any problems or learning barriers
- any supplementary study, or study support needs
- any matter of process, content or understanding raised by the students
- action to be taken in consequence.

In some programmes formal action planning may be appropriate.

Quite clearly this is a person-to-person activity. With present technology this may be more appropriately delivered by a centre-based tutor. However, broadband communications will open up face-to-face tutoring on-line and this will certainly help people in remote locations or who have restricted mobility.

Identifying support needs
The identification of support needs will flow from a number of the activities outlined above – in particular, appropriate tracking and monitoring of student activity, progress and achievement, the conduct of assessment tasks and various tutorial contents. What is important is that all of this information is monitored (if this can be

done automatically from student records, so much the better) and potential problems highlighted. In part, therefore, it is a question of system design.

This reinforces the need for guidance and support systems to be integrated into initial design of on-line learning programmes. A professional judgement of needs and appropriate actions will need to be made and appropriate support offered on this basis. The least this will require is a personal tutor-student link and possibly face-to-face communication (on- or off-line). Helping students to recognise support needs highlights the requirements on tutors to handle tutoring skilfully whether face-to-face or on-line. Refer to Chapter 7 for a more detailed discussion of these issues.

Achieving successful self-management

The goal of all guidance and support is to enable students to succeed as independent self-managing learners. Many adults will be able to bring these skills to their learning. There will be barriers, of using technology or developing skills for some. Younger learners often show a very wide range of confidence and skill in managing their learning.

A programme to develop and reinforce self-management will need to show some clear characteristics, based on good practice in more traditional forms of instruction.

- Support for self-management needs to be front-loaded so that learners can take control of their learning at their own speed. This will include:
  - full information that is required to understand the programme, recognise its demands, and to plan and schedule work
  - any training in the use of on-line systems and practising of relevant learning skills – for example, in a diagnostic assignment
  - direction to any support materials or activities which are necessary
  - establishing tutoring systems and support
- At the next stage proactive tutorial intervention will be necessary for learners who are identified through tracking and monitoring as having difficulties with

the programme or self-management. Help at this stage will include:

- review of learning, progress and difficulties
- help through action planning with scheduling of workload
- using feedback to help learners meet the demands of the programme
- teaching the requisite learning skills
- referral to support packages and activities.

This will require personal contact, however it is delivered. There is little evidence that many current on-line providers put this type of support fully into place. This contributes to the high drop-out rates in distance and on-line learning. Breaking learning into bite-sized chunks to some extent side-steps the problems, but if learners are to achieve meaningful accredited outcomes, many will need to pursue programmes of some substance.

Whether on-line learning is purchased on a purely commercial basis or with funding assistance from government, there is no justification to tolerate drop-out rates in excess of those for traditional delivery of similar provision through part-time or flexible study. The introduction of guidance and support to traditional programmes has had a substantial positive impact on retention and we should judge on-line learning by the same standards.

Once students have progressed through the initial stages, they will move towards full ability to manage their own learning successfully and demonstrate the learning skills appropriate to their level of study. Tutors will wish to keep students' development under review until they are fully confident.

Tutoring roles The discussion of developing learning reveals three complementary tutorial roles, which may be performed by one or more people.

    a. ***Front-line guidance and support*** covers base-level issues concerned with the use of technology, programme requirements, learning skills, queries and simple clarifications about the learning package. These are essentially realtime demands and require immediate guidance or support. They are fulfilled in a variety of ways according to their situations. For example, a learning centre may have general technical and tutorial support available to give the required tuition and guidance as the need arises. Alternatively, an on-line help desk or a telephone call centre can be used by larger providers to give the necessary guidance.

b. *Tuition* (in the sense of teaching), academic guidance on study requirements or learning strategies, feedback on assessment and more detailed programme and content queries can be answered on-line through asynchronous communication (via e-mail, in a newsgroup, web-based discussion or equivalent areas of virtual learning environment). Whilst students may appreciate a personal link or links here, these are tasks that can be carried out by a programme tutorial team, as long as attention is given to assuring consistency. These activities can be delivered with equal facility on- or off-line.

c. *Personal links* may be required where more proactive tutorial contact is needed from monitoring or providing structured periodic review. This is essentially concerned with learner management and may be achieved by:
   - designating a named link for these tasks
   - giving face-to-face contact.

	Learning centre tutor	Help desk	On-line tutor	Off-line or face-to-face support
Technical help	✓✓✓	✓✓		
Study support	✓✓✓		✓	✓✓
Teaching & tutoring			✓✓✓	✓✓✓
Tutorial review	✓✓		✓	✓✓✓

Table 6 Strategies for delivering support

One strategy is to designate a tutor at a learning centre to carry out these tasks. Not all students, however, will be able to attend learning centres due to work or family commitments, disability or geographical remoteness. Other strategies therefore need to be considered. Examples include using the telephone (not popular with some learners) or using broadband technology to give a realtime visual and voice link with a designated tutor. An alternative discussed below is to establish a mentoring system. This is particularly appropriate for work-based learners.

Mentoring and workplace support

On-line learning is particularly useful for people in remote situations or where working practices mean that centre-based study is inappropriate.

One way of providing some element of tutorial support is by designating workplace mentors. There is considerable literature and debate about mentoring and *Holloway and* the practice of mentoring. The role of the mentor *Whyte (1994)* cannot be the same as that of the tutor but, with training, mentors can deliver a number of key aspects of academic guidance including:

- sharing their own practice
- discussing areas of concern together
- challenging students' conceptions
- giving positive support
- giving honest feedback
- acting as a 'critical friend'.

Another possibility in the workplace is the development of peer support study circles, where a number of people are undertaking the same programme, or setting up pairs of 'learning buddies' (pairs of learners undertaking the same or similar programme). This can help to resolve many of the anxieties or perplexities of programmes and can give a degree of confidence to learners which they may not feel when working alone.

Mentoring on an industry-linked university course

Nottingham University has established an on-line postgraduate course in structure-based drug design. The students are scattered across the country working in various research laboratories. Since this area is at a frontier of development work, some student applications could be commercially sensitive.

The course provides on-line learning materials and some central tutoring direction. The most important tutorial element is a mentor from the student's own workplace, who can support the learning process and also tutor the student's work. Mentors are trained at Nottingham to undertake their role, and are in turn supported by course tutors.

This provision can make high quality learning materials available with local face-to-face support and commercial integrity preserved.

Summary

- On-line learning requires an integrated approach to teaching, guidance and support functions within the overall design of the learning programme.
- It is in the interests of both learners and providers to plan necessary elements of information and support to develop skills into learning programmes and help learners reflect on their own development.
- Strategies for managing learning will depend upon the nature of the provision.
- On-line tutors will be involved in a long list of detailed activities from tutoring discussions to achieving successful self-management, which form the centre of the support process.
- There are three complementary support roles concerned with front-line guidance, tuition and learner management, which may be carried out by one person or a team.
- Some support roles can also be delivered by a workplace mentor.

The next chapter looks at some of the organisational considerations in providing appropriate support.

Organising on-line learner support

Specific support may be necessary for students who experience disability or disadvantage. These ensure wider access. Support strategies are, however, appropriate to most learners to ensure that they achieve fully. Organisations should be clear about the support they offer. This chapter examines the process of identifying need, developing skills and providing support.

Supporting learning

Learner support systems ensure wider access and make sure that inclusive strategies are successful. In any area of education we need to make sure that students who are recruited are retained, helped to achieve and successfully complete their studies. This is as true of on-line learning as it is of any other mode of study.

On-line and distance learning have some advantages for many people who would otherwise be excluded from education. This includes those who face disabling barriers, as well as those who are geographically or socially isolated. They need to have the same chance of success as any other learner, however. This means having an infrastructure of support that gives them the opportunities equivalent to those that other students enjoy. It is also true that many other students will benefit from support, to help them achieve success more easily.

The danger is that on-line learning will offer very mechanical solutions to problems, which do not adequately meet needs. An approach which says in effect: 'learning difficulties – work through this pack' may or may not be a successful response. It will not meet the needs of many students. As with any other mode of provision a systematic process of needs identification and meeting these needs appropriately should be in place.

Identifying and meeting support needs

Bailey, Brown and Kelly (1996) Financial advice and debt counselling regulations now require services to undergo statutory registration to meet appropriate standards.

Not everything that influences a learner's performance can be dealt with by education providers and it is both right and appropriate that providers establish their boundaries for the help available. The Open University, for example, offers some counselling for learning problems and some advice on sources of finance, but would refer automatically to local counselling agencies for relationship issues. A residential university might offer at least initial guidance in all these areas, either through their student services or in association with their student union.

Other support requirements may be implied simply by the act of registering a student. Such areas might relate to the basic, key and learning skills needed to complete the course, or support for disability. In these cases, if a provider cannot give support, they should not take the enrolment.

Identifying support needs is therefore an essential part of student enrolment. The simplest and most effective system is self-declaration of learning difficulties or support needs to overcome disability. The anonymity of on-line self-declaration is helpful. It is essential, however, that before self-declaration is sought, policies on access and inclusion are made clear, the boundaries of support are established and the level of support available is apparent. Where learners are unsure, or their performance in initial assessment activities raises doubts, a link to diagnostic assessment instruments, as described in Chapter 5, may be required.

Support needs are many and various, but with on-line learning are most frequently going to fall into one of three categories:

- *Needs for technical support.* These can be resolved by an optional initial learning package for the software, by centre-based technical support, or by an on-line help desk.
- *Basic skills needs.* Some help can be given by referral to an appropriate basic skills learning package, although it is optimistic to think that there are universal solutions to basic skills learning needs that can easily be delivered by a supplementary package. There may be a need for more personal tutorial

support alongside the learning programme to provide step-by-step support and teaching.

- *Learning skills needs.* Again they may be tackled with a supplementary package. Developing learning skills is also, however, an essential function of tutoring for achievement and should be integral to the tutorial role.

Disability needs Beyond this will be more specialised needs, such as for students who face disabling barriers. Each student who declares a need in relation to disability should be given an individual assessment – thus ensuring equal access. Where the need is substantial, the assessment must be conducted face-to-face, together with liaison with other agencies who may provide relevant funding or professional services. For some areas of disability or disadvantage additional funding may be available from funding bodies for relevant learning programmes. This process is inevitably costly and time-consuming, but if inclusion and equal opportunity are to be taken seriously, it is a cost that has to be borne.

Supporting and developing skills In any programme of learning four sorts of skills are involved.

- *Subject-specific skills* are integral to the programme of learning (for example, book-keeping skills). In well written programmes, these will be developed systematically through learning and assessment materials.
- *General transferable skills* have a wide application in business, education and for personal development. These are normally referred to as key skills. They conventionally cover communications, numeracy, IT and problem solving.
- *Learning skills* are specific to study at any given level of education and type of programme. There may be some overlap between key skills and learning skills, but study/learning skills are generally more specific to the requirements of education. Another important difference is that, whilst key skills have always been seen as a fixed core of necessary abilities, learning skills are relative to the mode, level and area of study. Thus ability to take notes from lectures or

books is necessary for conventional study, whereas the ability to create, evaluate, check and manipulate data is essential for on-line study.

- ***Basic skills*** can be defined as the key skills of communication and numeracy at foundation level. Between 10% and 20% of adults have basic skills needs and if we are opening access to on-line learning, there will sometimes be a need to develop basic skills. Strategies that can deal with this are therefore required of the tutor.

It can be assumed that subject-specific skills will be embedded in any programme of learning. The difficulties become apparent with key skills and learning skills. What level of numeracy is assumed for an accountancy qualification, and therefore at what level should numerical techniques be taught? If we are opening access to study, what can we assume about the level of learning skills?

www. keyskillssupport.net

Welcome!

The Key Skills Support Programme is to help training providers, schools and colleges to improve quality of key skills provision and pave the way for the introduction of the new key skills programme from September 2000.

Baroness Blackstone, July 1999

- Click here for support for work-based training
- Click here for support for Schools and Colleges

Funded by the
Department for
Education and Employment

Figure 21 Key skills web site

There are two approaches to delivering key skills and learning skills. One is to deliver free-standing skills units and the second is to integrate the skills teaching into the learning programme and to map them across the learning activity to demonstrate coherence. There are arguments for and against each approach. The argument that supports integration is most persuasive when there is a fairly homogeneous intake to a long and demanding programme. In this circumstance, skills can be acquired in relation to specific learning tasks. For shorter, more flexible provisions, particularly with a disparate intake, it is preferable to offer additional skills support provision on an 'as needed' basis. This will be the case with many on-line programmes. Such programmes will often have available front-loaded optional packages which cover the necessary study skills.

There are, of course, some areas where the certification of key skills is mandatory. As more accredited programmes are offered on-line, there will be a need to offer key skills as part of any accredited programme of study. The decision on whether this is an integrated or free-standing element will need to be taken. In sixth form subjects key skills have moved from an integral element to a discrete one, although this may reflect administrative priorities more than educational ones. The modularity of most programme design is likely to argue for a free-standing unit.

Whichever route is taken, key and learning skills should be embedded throughout learning programmes. The essence of transferability is the ability to apply key skills, so the validity of accrediting key skills without assessing their application is questionable. That means that there should be points at which skills are applied and assessed in an explicit way. If skills development is integrated into learning programmes, it will also need to be integrated into on-line tutoring. Part of any on-line tutor's role is therefore to monitor and support the development of key and learning skills through the programme. The integrated assessment of key skills provides an essential vehicle for this. The outcomes of such an assignment can help to identify additional key skills/learning skills materials which should be introduced for those learners who require them.

In more dynamic systems, provision can be made for learners to claim key skills achievements on-line which, when achieved, can be entered in a Record of Achievement. This could allow a learner to inspect their progress record at any time (if suitably protected) and could allow tutors' and students' comments to be recorded on shared documents.

Where students have key skills development needs at foundation level, integrated delivery and assessment becomes more difficult. Basic skills development is generally treated in an individual way through a specific learning programme. This means that there needs to be a much more systematic focus for support, which will be covered in the next section.

Learner support Wider access means that learners who are disadvantaged or face disabling barriers should have equal opportunity to study alongside their peers. An essential part of this mission is to provide appropriate support, to enable learners to study on equal terms. There are two strands to this support. The first deals with disabilities and difficulties which can be overcome, but are not likely to be changed. These include loss of sight, hearing or mobility and some specific learning difficulties.

For learners with more severe visual, hearing or mobility barriers, on-line learning may be the ideal mode of provision. If they are to participate equally, a considerable but essential investment will need to be made to allow disabling barriers to be overcome. This can be achieved, for instance, by installing speech synthesis or other hardware or software adaptations and by providing software that will assist with particular learning needs. Technologies to assist these situations exist, but are rarely applicable 'off-the-shelf'. This is why

Refer to the section on identifying and meeting support needs an individual needs assessment and provision of the most appropriate software and hardware support should be made, including customisation for each learner.

It should be recognised that help can be given to a wide range of people, not just those with the most acute needs. For instance, slight hearing loss or uncorrected visual impairment can still create barriers to learning. These may not always be easily recognised.

Anna made poor progress at school, although it was obvious to her parents and teachers that she was articulate and had good verbal reasoning skills. She did not show signs of any of the usual learning difficulties, until a problem of visual co-ordination was diagnosed in her late teens. A combination of a change in prescription in her spectacles and a time allowance in examinations has enabled Anna to obtain a university degree and qualify as an accountant. Neither would have been achieved without special help. The visual correction allowed her to work easily on computers which is her preferred mode of study.

The second strand deals with disadvantages which have a social, economic or educational rather than physical base. As has been noted previously, a substantial proportion of the population has basic skills needs. This proportion has remained fairly constant over the past fifty years despite the many shifts in that time in schools' methodology. The reason, of course, is that it is not teaching methods that solve the problem (any one method will work for many children but not for all). The difficulty over the years has been in providing an appropriate range of teaching methods and in some schools concentrating specific and appropriate help on children in need. The fact is that, given specific help, children and adults do learn basic skills even when they have many disadvantages.

The development of appropriate basic skills packages on-line adds another tool to the armoury of basic skills teaching. Whilst it will not offer an educational panacea, it will provide a considerable extension to the strategies available. It does, of course, require some intensive personal support and help to self-manage learning from a tutor, particularly in the early stages. Students with basic skills needs often have broken schooling records, or have been demotivated or humiliated whilst at school. Although the availability of learning packages on-line is a very welcome development, they need to be used in a well supported context.

Peer and tutor There is a danger that support will be seen only in
support relation to particular needs and difficulties. It is not so
long ago that 'support' was accompanied by the adjective
'remedial' in higher education, which is odd given that
higher education usually selects successful learners. In
fact, all learners benefit from appropriate support. The
capable learner will need to be encouraged to take on
more demanding work, the less confident but able
learner to accept greater challenges. Indeed, support is
essential to learner management precisely because it
helps learners to extend themselves fully .

Support for average learners comes in a variety of
forms. One of the most important of these is peer
support. This is built in to the class or group structure of
traditional education. One of the very strong points
about virtual learning environments is that they can
provide for peer support in virtual coffee bars or similar
chat-room arrangements. This creates an on-line
equivalent of a learning group and is used skilfully by a
proportion of students. Others may choose to observe
the discussion, contributing less frequently.

Not all learners feel comfortable with this, so other
methods – such as learning circles – in which all
participants publish their work one to another, or setting
up group work on-line – can be used as strategies.
There are considerable advantages in ensuring that there
is tutor mediation, so that learning can be appropriately
managed. In one instance, however, students set up their
own private discussion space through an e-mail
subscription list, to discuss course matters away from
tutors – a clear indication that they owned and
controlled their learning!

Truly self-managing learners will also want to explore
possibilities beyond the boundaries of any particular
learning package. In institution-based learning,
discussions with tutors whether on- or off-line can be
quite easy to conduct, allowing individual exploration of
projects or assessment tasks. As discussed in Chapter 4,
however, many on-line and distance providers take a very
focused view of a subject which limits the range of
references and restricts scope for such exploration.
There is the danger of a limited and didactic view being
taken in many subject areas at both further and higher

education levels. The most capable students may wish to question and challenge, and programmes which cannot meet higher level tutorial demands will not fulfil the task of providing adequate tutoring support for these students. Provision for seminar space and debate is essential for longer and more ambitious programmes.

Support skills Tutoring is necessary for the development of learning skills and for personal development. All learning experiences affect both the personal and the knowledge base of the individual. Many developers of on-line learning tend to concentrate on the latter. A tutorial role can balance the two aspects. Tutoring for on-line learning means acquiring the skills to support the specific needs of the learner, in conjunction with the needs of the programme.

Undoubtedly, many good on-line programmes will incorporate learners' basic support needs – initial guidance on getting started, the skills to be developed, pointers for clarification, reinforcement of learning and anticipation of possible gaps in understanding. These may well be placed as additional to the main text, for example, through on-line help, or links to additional material.

Examples
'You may be wondering about . . . '
'At this point, you may like to select and read the following text file.'
'This might be a good place to stop and compare notes with others on the programme.'
'If you are in trouble here, e-mail your tutor (us!) and indicate your difficulties.'

The on-line tutorial will be proactive, anticipatory and show 'textual concern'. Such programmes can also build in reflection time to allow learning to be absorbed and health to be maintained (time away from the screen), for example, 'Take a 15 minute break here', 'Perhaps its time for coffee/tea', 'Reflect on what you have been doing' or 'What are the key themes that you have been working on.'

Tutoring for personal support and responding to specific needs is harder to accomplish through an on-line programme. This is when the role of a tutor assigned to learners is crucial, whether in a college, community provision or at the end of a phone or by e-mail. The role of such tutors includes:

- checking that needs are being met and that the students are capable of achievements on the chosen programme
- ensuring that the level is right for each individual learner; this will require listening to past learning experiences, that make up each individual's 'learning history'
- discussing learners' preferred approach to learning. How does this match with the programme requirements? If there is no choice of approach, then how can the learner be helped to cope with the demands of the programme?
- providing advice on approaches, developing or recommending study guides
- being available regularly for support (in person or on-line) as appropriate
- checking on progress and achievement and agreeing times for review
- keeping a student going when the learning process hits difficulties, and anticipating when this might be; this may require thorough knowledge of a package, or the development of a manual for tutors by the writer of the learning packages indicating possible bumps and leaps in knowledge/skills within the programme
- giving feedback on progress and reviewing further options
- referring on to other kinds of support/help as appropriate for the individual
- checking on completion and progression.

Learning on-line is about being empowered to gain new understanding. Widening opportunities and participation in learning should include support that leads to empowering the learner. In fact, tutor dependency is not helpful in delivering on-line learning, so the skills of self-learning and coping strategies have to be built into the process.

Empowerment v dependency

Empowering support
- Affirms what learners can already do
- Encourages learners to identify their own problems
- Deals with feelings of helplessness
- Involves listening and 'reading between the e-mail lines'
- Respects learners' rights to decide how they will proceed
- Encourages reflection on the learning experience.

Dependency support
- Does everything for the students
- Rescues people ('Let me sort out where you should be on the screen')
- Confirms feelings of inadequacy ('This is a complicated programme to use!')
- Gives advice: for example, 'If I were you . . . '
- Concentrates on the learning content, not the learner
- Makes decisions for the learner.

Negotiating

Tutors will always use the skills of negotiation with learners. For on-line learning this means helping individuals agree their learning goals, and helping them organise their time and approach and plan the learning process with an acceptable time-frame. A tutor may need to negotiate on behalf of a learner in order to ensure specific support is available for individual needs (larger screen monitor/scribe/extra time).

Negotiating with learners requires the further skill of empathy. This means communicating to learners an understanding of how they are feeling. This is not easy as an on-line tutor, but as the Samaritans now offer e-mail support, it is not impossible to use such a system to help support personal difficulties that relate to the learning needs.

Tips for empathy (on- and off-line)
- Keep responses short (they can be frequent in a crisis but concise/supportive).
- Make language empathic (respond to the learners' language styles, use some of their words in reply).

- Respond to the learners' voice tones, if speaking; this means putting your own emotions 'on hold'.
- Give yourself time to think (e-mail replies can be composed more carefully).

Tutoring support for on-line learning may require the skill of helping learners cope with change. In a further education college, learners who are used to a pastoral approach to personal tutoring may find that on-line tutoring now has a stronger emphasis on recording achievement and planning learning steps through action plans. It is in the learners' interests to ensure that they are able to access time to discuss concerns about learning related to personal issues or learning blocks, such as anxiety about on-screen testing. It is the organisation's concern to ensure that support for individual needs is available in some form, either on- or off-line.

Making sense of learning is about making sense of experiences. Tutorial and learning support has a role in helping with this process. Many learners will need help, not just in acquiring the skills of on-line learning, but in coping with the 'knock-on' effects this will have on their own perceptions of the learning process. Tutoring for on-line learning also means being confident that the support will work for the learner. If the tutor is hesitant, the learner will react to this uncertainty and this could lead to an unhappy learning experience. Tutors must have worked through their own process of accommodating to changes, modifying, rejecting and revising the structure. Any system of dissemination of knowledge can, of course, be regarded with relative detachment: the tutor does not have to be emotionally committed but must be professionally committed to delivering the approach.

Giving information on how to get started, what to do or what is available to learn will in itself bring about changes in approach. It has to be accompanied by support that is committed to offering a secure zone (on- or off-line) within which the learner can accommodate their own sense of themselves and develop their own internal resources, and that will provide confidence in themselves as learners in order to complete their studies successfully.

Remember when tutoring:

- In order to help someone it is not always necessary to understand why they have a learning barrier.
- Learners often have more resources than they think.
- Learners make the best choices if they can own their decisions.
- Some people find a change of approach threatening.
- Age, class and ethnic origin do not have any implications on the ability to change, learn or manage programmes and empathy can help to deliver relevant provision.
- If the learner feels powerless, this can spiral into meaningless and pointless and may end with the learner dropping out of the programme.
- Most learners will need support to plan their progress and find useful ways to complete their goals.
- On-line learners need reassurance that help is available when they need it and should be clearly contracted at the beginning of the tutor–learner relationship.

Summary

- Learner support systems ensure wider access. It is essential, however, that support is appropriately based on the needs of the learner.
- Many learners benefit from support to develop the skills that help them to succeed.
- Providers should be clear about what support they can provide and how they identify it.
- Students who face disabling barriers will need more detailed assessment and specific support.
- Support for developing learning and key skills can be either delivered through free-standing units or integrated in the main programme.
- The learning group and the tutor both provide support and this can be repeated on-line.
- On-line tutoring will be proactive, anticipatory and empowering. It will use negotiation and empathy to help learners overcome barriers.

Implementing the future

This book has argued for the central place of guidance and support processes for on-line learning. It has suggested that this is best achieved through integrated programme design and has discussed the requirements for effective integration. This chapter summarises the content of this book into a checklist for implementation.

The future is here

For good or ill an irreversible process of change is occurring in education. There is much that is good in this process. The flexibility with which education can be delivered will allow much greater accessibility to sustain lifelong learning. Students will have better access to information, whether held on institutional intranets, within new on-line learning programmes or on the world wide web.

In particular, the business of information giving will be revolutionized. Some provision will adopt a more programmed approach to teaching and learning, with learning broken into bite-sized chunks, each carefully staged and assessed, to ensure acquisition of knowledge and understanding. Other provision, particularly in academic subjects and at a higher level, may require greater student self-management of information retrieval and analysis, probably structured by a programme of formative and summative assessment.

There are dangers, however. Some approaches to on-line learning may become much more didactic in form and content. Chapter 3 instanced approaches to computer training that do not generally constitute desirable models for on-line learning, and Chapter 4 showed the potential narrowing of academic debate and the knowledge domain. On the other hand, the expansion of spurious information available on the web is also illustrated in Chapter 4.

A discussion of valid and bogus provision can be found at www.degree.net/ guides.html

Let us be clear that both didacticism and misinformation will undermine the liberal educational agenda which aims to produce a well-informed population, able to analyse and evaluate opinion and information and form evaluative and critical interpretations leading to action. There are many people in politics, business, education and the media who would find it convenient to roll back the liberal agenda to produce a population that knows what it is taught and does what it is told. For these people, just as much as liberal educators, the coming revolution in education is an opportunity and they have at least as much access to the levers of power as the liberal establishment.

If we wish education to continue to provide the critical tools upon which effective democracy relies, then we have to ensure that they are incorporated into on-line learning. Critical tools are taught not by instruction but through discussion and practice. They rely disproportionately on human interaction and as we establish on-line learning, we need to identify and implement the equivalents of this within the design of on-line programmes.

This book has argued that tutoring, which is seen to embrace teaching, guidance and support activities, is the central activity in developing learning, together with related learning and critical skills. The book also embraces the need for full information about the form, structure and content of learning. It is the simple principles of giving full information and developing learning (the elements of which are identified in Chapter 2) which can be used to guide the implementation of support for on-line learning.

An implementation programme

The next part of this section provides a brief summary of the necessary support structure and how it may be implemented for on-line learning. Not all of this will be relevant to the whole range of provision from an institutional intranet to a virtual learning environment, as the support structure will vary depending on the type of provision. The main activities will, however, be common to all systems.

Initial guidance and support
Figure 16 page 65

Pre-entry information and guidance
It is a straightforward matter to set up a website to provide a range of information, as shown in Figure 16. Course information should be sufficiently detailed to give the principle objectives, content, activities, assessment requirements and outcomes. General facilities, finance,

fees and contacts for further information should also be covered. A virtual campus tour is useful for international students or those at a distance from teaching institutions.

Educational and careers guidance

There are a number of packages that can give a general indication of aptitudes and interests which could be either used on-line or downloaded. Many people, however, prefer the live interactions given by face-to-face or at least telephone contact. Broadband communication may allow this at a distance. Educational and careers guidance should conform to the criteria laid out in Chapter 2.

Application and selection

On-line application is appropriate in many situations within further education, distance learning and the university clearing phase. It is clear from inspection reports that students who visit a provision and are interviewed prior to selection are more likely to be retained. Both parties can be sure that the provision is appropriate. Telephone interviews or local agents are often used for international students. Again, broadband communication may improve the quality of contact.

Induction

Whilst traditional induction will continue for institution-based students, direct equivalents can be easily developed as HTML pages on-line. It is important to match the scale to the duration of the programme, but on-line materials might cover the use of the intranet, learning technology, course information, tutorial support and access to learning resources.

Assessment of skills and support requirements

The most widely used tool is a diagnostic assignment, usually included in the induction period. The Open University often uses an initial assignment which links the students' own experience to the topic under consideration. This can be used to identify support needs and areas for development through learning. The simplest level of additional provision is self-declaration of support needs, with use of specialist self-diagnostic tests, or a full diagnostic test as back-up. Suitability for entry to a programme is better determined at selection stage – diagnosis should concentrate on support needs.

Guidance and support through the programme

The ideal model will encompass the tutoring and support activities given in Figure 8 (page 29) through the guidance stages that are outlined in Table 3b (page 39). These can also be applied to the learner-centric model of education developed in Figure 2 (page 9) which provides a useful framework for considering how support can be implemented and embedded.

Curriculum design, content and organization

It has been argued throughout the book that guidance and support should be integrated into the design of curriculum and teaching.

Access to the curriculum

On-line learning should enable greater flexibility, particularly in relation to when and where study is undertaken. Wholly on-line learning can be conducted through an institutional learning centre, distributed to a community learning centre or accessed remotely from the home or workplace. The integration of support can be achieved by appointing a front-line support worker in learning centres to answer technical queries and questions about the learning packages. Access to tutors, either face-to-face or remotely by e-mail or telephone, is necessary for academic guidance. In distance learning front-line queries may be handled by a call centre and

Refer to Chapters 3 and 4

further academic guidance by on-line tutors or workplace mentors.

Access to the curriculum for those with disabilities or learning difficulties needs to be carefully implemented as discussed in Chapter 7.

Mode of study

Producing on-line materials of quality is costly and time-consuming and is also expensive to purchase. Unless distance/distributed learning is a necessity, the major use of on-line materials may be to create a learning environment on an intranet to hold materials supporting teaching and learning. This will give the opportunity to switch resources from instruction to consolidating learning through tutoring and add greater flexibility benefiting from the uses of technology (for example, e-mail or on-line discussion) without incurring the major costs of production and on-line support. In distance and distributed learning the method of support for learning packages is a crucial consideration.

Curriculum organization and design

The design and content of the curriculum needs to be carefully considered if teaching is to be conducted on-line. For instance, an on-line learning package may cover in a number of hours of interactive study the same material as a few pages of a book. The book is more efficient at giving information, the learning package more efficient at consolidating learning.

From the point of view of the learner, the optional position might have been to read the pages, prepare some notes in answer to questions on them and to have engaged in realtime discussion in a seminar or on-line activities taking, at the most, a couple of hours and integrating tutorial support. Strategies which reduce teaching costs are not necessarily the most efficient for learners' time.

Investment will need to be put into the on-line curriculum to ensure that it stays up to date. Once again, the cost and benefits in fast-moving or specialised areas may be to create a resource base rather than a teaching programme on-line, unless, like the example taken from Nottingham University, there are overriding geographical or commercial reasons to do so.

Teaching, learning and assessment

Managing learning

Learners are challenged most effectively through varied learning experiences. Learning packages have their place for particular tasks or short programmes. The variety of experience which can be given in a virtual learning environment is more likely to allow the development of learning. Integrated tutoring to manage students' progress through the work, manage discussions and give academic guidance is necessary. These are equivalent to those deployed in traditional learning, although they may use electronic communication at a distance.

Learning skills

Attention needs to be paid to the development of learning skills together with critical and analytical skills. These are developed largely through discussion and application in assignments tasks with tutorial management, guidance and feedback. This can be achieved equally well using electronic communication.

Key skills may need to be integrated into the programme and opportunities for demonstrating and claiming skills competence will need to be provided.

Assessment

A variety of on-line assessment techniques can be used for self-checking, providing computer-based formative feedback and stage tests. Examination of the knowledge base can also be conducted through on-line assessment techniques. Demonstration of higher levels of competence and the ability to practise higher order intellectual skills and apply knowledge and understanding for accredited programmes requires systems of off-line assignment or application work, which may be submitted on-line.

Crucial questions for support are the speed with which feedback is given together with quality and completeness. Minimum standards of entitlement, such as feedback to be given within ten working days and standardised instruments relating feedback to learning outcomes and assessment criteria, are desirable.

Student progression and achievement

Tracking and monitoring

For all longer on-line learning programmes, systems which monitor activity, track and monitor progress and report at regular intervals (weekly, for example) to a tutor who is managing the learning are essential. Retention is aided by early identification of students at risk and immediate, proactive, guidance and support should be given.

Reviewing progress

Review is an essential tool for managing learning and giving guidance and support. Again, it is best conducted at regular intervals whether it is on- or off-line. On-line programmes should indicate review points and arrange review times by e-mail. Review should include formative feedback, reflection by the learner and action planning of targets and activities for the next period. This is a realtime activity whether conducted face-to-face or on-line.

Recording achievement

Tracking systems can be used to maintain a record of achievement, including units passed, key skills competences claimed and accredited and level of performance. Such a record, as well as providing a summative statement of progress, is a basis for review, feedback and academic guidance.

Student support and guidance Diagnostic assessment, academic guidance and learning support are considered fully in Chapters 5, 6 and 7. These should be integrated into other aspects of provision as this discussion shows. Diagnostic assessment should be approached at the initial guidance stage. Academic guidance, along with other learning management activities, is best delivered through an active tutoring system, which is also able to provide front-line support through review, action planning and careful feedback on the development of learning and related skills. Additional support systems may be required for students with basic skills needs, identified disabilities or learning difficulties.

Learning resources *Access*

Support for access may be necessary for those with disabilities as discussed in Chapter 7. The aim of on-line learning is to make access to learning resources flexibly available when required by the learner. Access to the intranet/learning environment is therefore essential over-night and at weekends, which poses some problems for technical maintenance.

Usage

It is necessary to ensure that resources are widely accessed and used by students. This applies whether the resource is a supplementary handout available on-line or software package to embed tables and graphs in assignment work. Students may need to be trained to use resources.

Adequacy

Resource adequacy relates to the demands of curriculum and tutoring and raises questions of diversity, relevance and currency which mirror those discussed in relation to the curriculum.

Quality management and enhancement

Quality management

Control quality by setting a minimum entitlement for the provision of tutoring and support activities.

Responding to student feedback

Regular opportunities to evaluate and provide feedback on learning programmes should be given, leading to improvements which are fed to students.

Responding to examiner and verifier feedback

This requires regular (for example, annual) review in relation to feedback, retention and outcomes achieved.

Quality control of assessment

Implement rigorous processes to assure appropriate assessment and the integrity of marking.

Quality enhancement

Review of provision should be developmental, leading to improvement through planned development of the content and delivery of provision. Training for tutors, linked to their developmental needs, should be established through effective appraisal systems.

Guidance for progression

This can be divided into two parts. The first is essentially a tutorial function, reinforcing activities and skills which are relevant for progression. This may include the encouragement to produce and update CVs, arranging work-related guidance, supporting periods of placement or work-related study. Such careers-related education should be embedded in curriculum learning materials and activities.

Further information on books on implemention can be found at www.lpbooks.co.uk.

The second is education and careers guidance. Tutors may be qualified for supporting educational progression (for example, the university application process) but careers guidance is best achieved through referral to careers guidance specialists.

Bibliography

Adapt (1999) *Survey by Learning Partners for Adapt – Learners at Work Project* Gloucestershire 1999

Bailey, D., Brown, J. and Kelly, P. (1996) *Academic Advice, Personal Counselling and On-programme Guidance in the Open University* in: *Personal Tutoring and Academic Advice* HEQC 1996

Bartram, D (1999) *Computer Based Testing to Assess Students' Potential* Inform Issue 2 FEDA

BTEC (1993) *Staying the Course* Business and Technician Education Council

Davies, D (2000) Times Educational Supplement (29.9.00)

Employment Department (1991) *Definitions of a Gateway Service*

Entwhistle, N (1992) *The Impact of Teaching on Learning Outcomes* in: *Higher Education – a Literative Review* CVCP

Fage and Heron (1990) *Counselling in the British Open University* in: D. Bailey et al (Eds) *Personal Tutoring and Academic Advice* HEQC 1996

Gow, L and Kember D (1993) *Conceptions of Teaching and Learning and their Relationship to Student Learning* British Journal of Educational Psychology, 63 (1)

Guardian Educational Supplement 19th September 2000

Hall C. and Corney R. (1995) *Students who Withdraw from their First Year of Studies* Unpublished monograph University of Greenwich, Department of Psychology

Hatton, A and Sedgemoor, L (1992) *Marketing for College Managers* The Staff College, Blagdon

HEFCE (1995/6) *Teaching and Learning Technology Programme* TLTP Catalogues Spring 1995, Spring 1996 HEFCE

Hennessy S., Flude M. and Tait A. (1999) *Open University, School of Education Research* reported in *Sesame* August/ September 1999

HESA (1999) *Performance Indicators in Higher Education* Higher Education Statistics Agency 99/66

Holloway, A. and Whyte, C. (1994) *Mentoring – the Definitive Workbook* Development Process Publications/ Swansea College

Honey, D. and Mumford, L. (1986) *Using Your Learning Styles* Ardingley House

Hurley, J. (1994) *Supporting Learning* Learning Partners/Further Education Staff College

Hurley, J., Smith, J. and Hurley, L. (1995) *Tutoring for Achievement – Frameworks* Learning Partners/FEDA

IT Training (1999) Research carried out for the DfEE by the Epic Group reporting in *IT Training* June 1999

NCET (1988) *Computer Aided Guidance Evaluation* National Council for Educational Technology

Offer, M. (1998) *Information Technology in Careers Education and Guidance: an Historical Perspective* in: M. Crawford et al (Eds) *Taking Issue, Debates in Guidance and Counselling in Learning* Routledge

QAA/HEFCE (1998) *Subject Assessment Overview Report for Land and Estate Management* QAA

QAA (1999) *Annual Report 1998/99* QAA

Saunders, G (2000) *Getting Started With On-Line Learning* Learning Partners

Smith, J. and Hurley, L. (1996) *Tutoring for Achievement – Skills* Learning Partners/FEDA

Times Educational Supplement 15th September 2000

UDACE (1986) *The Challenge of Change* Unit for the Development of Adult Continuing Education

Watts, A (1995) *Computers and Guidance* in: A. Watts et al (Eds) *Rethinking Careers Education and Guidance* Routledge

www.open.ac.uk/experience
www.chelt.ac.uk
www.keyskillssupport.net
www.learn2.com
www.polemicpublishing.co.uk
http://comentor.hud.ac.uk/
www.ferl.co.uk
www.learndirect.co.uk
http://www.qmark.com
www.virtualuniversity.ac
www.fastrack-consulting.co.uk
www.abacustraining.co.uk
www.degree.net
www.lpbooks.co.uk

Also from Learning Partners

The Managing On-line Learning series will continue to produce resources which enable staff in schools, further and higher education to engage with the coming revolution in learning. The series, through its various titles deals with both the strategy and practice of on-line learning. The aim is to help teachers approach on-line learning in a reasoned and informed way. Each publication places the learner and the teacher, rather than the technology, at the centre.

Already available:

Getting Started with on-line learning.
Gunter Saunders
ISBN 1 899692 06 1